LOVE ONLY

LOVE ONLY

KAVITA GUPTA

JAICO PUBLISHING HOUSE

Ahmedabad Bangalore Bhopal Chennai
Delhi Hyderabad Kolkata Lucknow Mumbai

Published by Jaico Publishing House
A-2 Jash Chambers, 7-A Sir Phirozshah Mehta Road
Fort, Mumbai - 400 001
jaicopub@jaicobooks.com
www.jaicobooks.com

LOVE ONLY
ISBN 978-93-90166-28-2

First Jaico Impression: 2021

Page design and layout: Inosoft Systems, Delhi

To,

Mom and Dad

When the mind falls in love, it's temporary;
When the heart falls in love, it lasts a lifetime;
When the soul falls in love, it's eternal.

Spiritual League

Foreword

This book is meant for the incorrigibly romantic, written by a romantic herself! For the absolute romantics, pure love exists only in their relationship with God. Or it exists in their mind, where it can never be consummated. The moment pure love is tainted by a carnal thought or act, it starts a stopwatch, which determines love's eventual demise.

The book traces the journey of a beautiful angel, who is God's favourite. She basks in a benign all-encompassing cloud of never-ending love, but she has a human gene imbedded in her perfect life. So she feels a human ache to feel the intense pleasure and pain, which she feels is missing in her perfect world! Restless and unhappy, she requests God to let her go to the world of humans. After a lot of gentle soul-searching, he relents and sends her to the imperfect world of humans so that she can begin her odyssey to search for her perfect lover.

This story will resonate with all those looking for their perfect love and soulmates. The journey can be quite a roller-coaster ride—read on!

Prahlad Kakkar
Ad Film Director

Acknowledgments

I am truly indebted to all those who have deeply touched my life, facilitating its exciting journey through waves and tides of circumstance.

It is said that parents are the first gurus. I acknowledge the ever-present commitment of my parents to my happiness, as they made every possible sacrifice for my sake. My mother almost passed away when I was born and has since lived precariously. She has worked overtime to ward off any harm coming my way. Because I was a difficult child, I have seen my father constantly exasperated, but he overcame all his frustration as time passed. I remember my mother relate the story, several times, of the Rajput queen 'Hadi Rani' who beheaded herself because the king returned again and again to bid her farewell while setting out to the battlefield. My father, who retired as a Major General in the Indian Army, was passionately dedicated to his service for the nation. I learnt the fervour of duty from both my parents and this strong call of duty for the country and the people has been the abiding principle of my life. It has taken a front seat even as I do realize that in this pursuit, I have been occasionally callous to my family and friends.

I was also blessed to have my sister as my second guru. Amita guided me through my childhood and adolescent years, which were difficult for me in every way. I was not a happy child and

Amita was like my second mother, a source of security. Her loving support, my father's strength and my mother's unfailing soothing care are the foundation of my academic achievements. I would be failing in my duty if I did not mention the affection and support of Amita's husband, Dr. Sanjeev Rastogi.

I acknowledge the loving contributions of my wonderful elder sister, Dr. Smita Chugh, and her magnificent husband, Arvind Chugh, both top bureaucrats, and my seniors in the IAS, who have done yeoman service for the country. Arvind Chugh, the former Chief Secretary, Government of Jharkhand, also helped me proofread this book.

Soon after I entered the Civil Services, during my probation period, I met Pinak Pani Prasad Sharma, the Superintendent of Police, Wardha. The synchronicity of such events is only ever pre-ordained. As soon as I met him, I knew he would play an important role in my life. He and his wife, Indira *didi* gave me a home away from home. He has understood me more comprehensively than anyone else. He has been instrumental in my survival through the long years when the eternal problem of my life was 'To be or not to be.'

Coincidentally, during this time, I also met my first spiritual guru, the late Dr. Rajaram Deshpande. My association with him was deeply enriching to my soul. I was at *gurukul* when I was with him and did my *tapasya*; I have never experienced such spiritual peace as I did in his presence. He taught me the *Bhagavad Gita*, the Celestial Song of the Universe, and *Patanjali's Yoga Sutra*. He was a source of great inspiration. I think I would have been saved much anguish had I stuck to my spiritual agenda with my spiritual guru, rather than get embroiled in worldly life.

Nonetheless, my second spiritual guru, Chaudhary Uncle, believed that my spiritual journey would be refined only after I enter *samsar*. That's how I entered *samsar* and got married. My marriage taught me an important lesson, which I would not have learnt otherwise. I understood I am not the 'doer,' I am a pawn and the game of chess is being played elsewhere. Inayat taught me patience, forbearance and many family values. He gave me freedom to do my work with devotion and allowed me to do full justice to my duties. He has also been my guru in many ways. Through him, I also met masters like Ahad Sahab in Kashmir.

I met Chariji and my present master, 'Daaji,' thereafter and have been practicing the 'Heartfulness Way' ever since. The path through the heart is always the most direct one. It is also the shortest way to the ultimate. I deeply acknowledge their presence in my life.

My spiritual journey continues, as I continue to meet and know masters like Om Swami, Patriji and Dr. Newton.

I am immensely grateful to Dr. Pradeep Jain who has been special in many ways.

I am thankful to Sumit Mullick, the former Chief Secretary, Government of Maharashtra, who has critically reviewed my book despite his tight schedules.

I am forever indebted to Dr. Rajendra Singh for his invaluable help in enabling this book to see the light of day.

I am thankful to Karishma Chhatrapati for her help in editing this book.

I also acknowledge the presence of my dear friends and batchmates from IIT Delhi; and from WTI, Berne, Switzerland; of my IAS colleagues and batchmates; and of all my co-practitioner brothers and sisters in the Sahaj Marg and the Sangha who have enriched my life variously.

Just as salt adds so much taste to food, there are people who have added so much to my life. I am privileged to know them and cognizant of all the support extended by them to me, and I immensely value the same.

In my journey through Hinduism, Christianity, Buddhism, *Vipassana*, Islam, Sufism, and now the 'Heartfulness Way,' I have encountered masters who have guided me. Despite the best guidance, I still find myself at crossroads. I hope the journey will become simpler and purer with the passing of the days. I can already feel the magic happening.

Dr. Kavita Gupta

Contents

Contents

chapter 1

Creation

One day, in his dream,
God spoke,
"The Word" was the beginning

With the beginning, he felt proud,
He revelled
And, in his pride, embers lit,
Stars and fire flew,
God called man and gave fire.

Each man carried this fire within him,
As fire burned within,
God suffered.
This suffering felt good
He called it love.

With fire and love within man,
God paused,
This was the beginning of doubt.

God told man,
"I have felt all these emotions for you

And I owe them to you."
God was kind.

His kindness gave rise to his first blessing
And the first prophet was born.
God was pleased.
In his pleasure, he gave man a reward,
Hope was born.

Now, God looked at his creation,
He liked it.
God commanded his creation to balance
Fire, love, doubt and hope.
Man was perplexed.

To help him,
God gave him faith.
"Faith," he said, "will redeem you."
To operate it,
He created space and time.

When God created all this,
He felt happy.
In his happiness, he smiled.
This was God's grace to humankind!

chapter 2

Desire

She looked at him in awe and wonder, she loved him. She looked at his creation and then again at him. Everything was perfect and perfectly programmed, so perfect that she could see the end in the beginning and the beginning in the end. It cycled endlessly, and all the emotions, good and bad, perfectly balanced each other. God smiled, she saw the love in his eyes, a love that was eternal and a love that only a creator could have for his creation. This made her jealous.

"What is your dream?" God asked.

She replied, "Lord! I know you love me, but I also know you love the stars and the planets, the galaxies, the sun and the moon. You love space and time. You love every being that exists, big and small. You love the cruel and the kind equally. You even love the unjust as you love the just. You love the sinner as you love the saint. You love them all because you are the Creator; however, I feel lost. You love me just as much as you love the other angels, or even the imps. I wonder, what is the difference between your love for me and your love for others?"

With every glance God bestowed upon her, her desire to be loved exclusively became stronger and more intense. She continued, "Lord, you have created me. I am always at your service, looking after all your needs. Yet, I feel this is to no avail. I wonder, if I did none of this like many who don't, would you still love me as much?"

God looked at her and smiled. Even though the angel could not understand the meaning of his smile, she understood that he knew her desire.

God knew the seed of her desire was the want for human love. "You seek a love that is exclusive. You seek a mirage. You are like the fragrant deer that chases its own fragrance to the ends of the jungle and falls asleep tired of the search. Do you know the fate of the *kasturi* deer?" He asked her compassionately.

"It ultimately discovers that the fragrance is within its own body and its search ends," the angel replied.

"No, that never happens! It runs and runs till it falls dead or till it is found by someone who is in search of the fragrance that it carries. When it dies, it is the most unfulfilled creature."

"Alas! It searches for what it carries within!" she exclaimed.

"Do you know how the men in the world treat the *kasturi* deer when it is found?" God asked.

"Humans take it home so that it fills the space within the four walls with the fragrance they love. Surely, they give the deer all their love and attention," she replied confidently.

"No, that does not happen. When the *kasturi* deer is found, it is shot dead. The pouch of fragrance is extracted and its flesh is eaten. Its skin is stretched and made into a carpet on which men walk," God revealed.

The angel protested in disbelief, "That is cruel! Lord, what do you do when you see your creation treat another this way? Surely your heart bleeds."

"I am beyond the good and bad. These are the ways of the world. I created the *kasturi* deer for a purpose. It is a reminder to all of my creation that the object of their search is always within. The curse of desire is a subtle ignorance of the mind. It is part of the human journey to go through the churning of desire to dispel ignorance and come into pure love."

"Do you know why you seek love?" God asked his dear angel.

"I seek it because that is my mission," the angel replied.

"Yes, it is your mission, and you seek it because of the love within you. Not everyone seeks love. Do you know why people are dazzled by gold and why more wars are fought for gold than for anything else?" he enquired.

"Because gold is rare and it shines brightly," came her prompt reply.

"The search for gold is because every creature is conceived in the golden womb—the *hiranya garbha.* That dazzling gold is the source of all creation and an innate part of it; that alone is the real gold. All gold that is outside is an illusion, all that is created with ignorance is not the real and is attracted to the falsehood of illusions," he explained. After a brief pause, he asked, "Why does everybody seek happiness?"

"This I know! Happiness is within," she whooped. Then, she thought for a moment and with a breath of gentle exasperation she continued, "But Lord, if happiness is within, there should be no search... or is it that the search occurs precisely because it is within everyone and everyone is ignorant about its presence?"

God cautioned her, "Time and again, all this has been revealed in different ways in the scriptures of all religions and by prophets and saints. Men know this intellectually but their heart cannot perceive it; layers of wanton desires bury it. The law of karma does not allow them to shed their ignorance easily. Even if they know this, their knowledge does not lead them to enlightenment. Humans are condemned by their own habits. The habits make grooves in the human psyche till one day, they slip into them. Habits give rise to desires. You see these men caught up in their own desires? They lull themselves into a stupor and suffer."

"My precious one," God continued his caution. "You must stop these discriminatory thoughts because they stem from attachment. Attachment causes desire, anger, craving and misery."

Satan, who was observing this dialogue between God and his angel, seemed a little uncomfortable in his seat. God turned to Satan and said, "Even you are my very own. One day you too shall return to me. I am your purpose. Every action of yours steers human beings closer to me. Though you are my dearest and nearest, I banished you because you were overcome by your own pride. Yet, remember, I gave you the boon of my eternal presence. Where you are, I am. I gave you a boon and I told you, you shall be wherever I am."

God revealed to Satan:

Men shall reach me only through thy touch!
This is my boon to thee, my son,
A boon, known to none!

Thou shalt never be far from me.
Nor by space, nor time,
Nor even by essence,
Nor less great.

Experiencing thee,
Will my presence be.
Man will falter when he is weak,
My grace then he shall seek.

Thy eyes that glaze like green
Shall delude many of their gleam.
With suffering that thou shall create,
Thou art destined to recreate.

With Thy touch all their longings profane,
Shall heavenly pleasures feign.
Yet slowly, bleeding, all shall pass in vain.

Thou shalt then descendeth with an uncanny pain,
Men and women shall writhe in anger and disdain.

In flames thou shalt consign,
All dreams that children sign,
Yet, I shall return to the kind,
Gold within, that they would find.

With all thy might,
Thou shalt kill the right,
But with my sight,
Man shall see the light!

Thou shall frame a cross,
To crucify me, with a toss.
Yet, with my design,
To dust, you shall resign.

Dust to fire,
Fire to rocks,
Resounding a music,
Rivers rushing on rocks.

The dead would rise affirming me,
Conquering hearts with love of me.

A thousand times more great,
They shall stand tall and straight,
Lording over a wisdom new,
As sun shines over the brew.

With all hell unleashed by you,
Man shall be as was never due.
Reversing all pain and rancour,
Equalling me, like never before!

The angel understood that Satan and his army are the will of God, only there to hasten the spiritual journey of man.

Despite this, the angel was afflicted by obsession. She heard all that God spoke to her and Satan, yet she listened to nothing. She knew what God said to Satan was a message for her, gently cautioning her from seeking her desire. Every parent knows that the path ahead is strewn with thorns. Yet, there is nothing a stubborn child understands when desire clouds innocence. The parent also knows that the lessons will educate the child and their love will always heal the wounds.

The angel looked at the world that glittered from a distance. She surveyed the horizon with her telescopic eyes. God saw her gazing intently and marvelled. Sensing his presence, Anjali revealed what she saw.

Focusing my vision,
Scanning through a million revisions
I scan across time and galaxies.

I rest my eyes on one on high,
In a lovely light through the sky.
Shining, in a castle standing tall,
A thousand princes and princesses at his call.

I see a man, and his face
All handsome,
And full of grace.

I see a concern in his eyes,
A longing in his sighs.
An elegance, a demeanour,
A boyish mischief.

I feel a strange attraction luring me,
As if a distant music is calling me.

Across aeons and miles I smile,
As time draws a boundary and distance curls.

From stories that I heard,
I know a shepherd he is, for his herd.

I see in a sudden fate,
He flying me on a Persian carpet.
He performs for me his magical prowess,
Touching stars, melting rocks, ringing bells,
Churning melodies from seashells.

I think I like him,
Nay, I love him!
I crave for him,
For, certain I am, I want to be with him.

She had heard tales of great love and she wanted to experience it. She told God, "You are the Creator and you must love all your beings equally. Your love can never be only for me. I want to experience that love by someone whose love is not shared. This is my desire."

God lovingly told his angel, "If you wish for the love of a human, you cannot be loved as long as you remain an angel with wings. Everyone has the right to dream and search for it, so be it with you. May the winds carry my touch when you need me the most."

chapter 3

Birth

The planets had been cast in their positions, marking the blueprint of Anjali's life. Anjali was born. She was experiencing the trauma of birth.

At birth, a sudden realization dawns that the soul has descended into a new conceptual space. Birth in a particular place may seem like an accident. However, it is one's karmic legacy that causes the birth in the here and now. It is a legacy carried forward from each past life, and it also projects the future lives to come.

When the soul emerges and acquires the body, it interfaces with the external world to realize a reality that is not safe. It realizes that it is on its own and gasps for the first breath, the first inhalation at birth. This first breath calms the self as the experience of the world around penetrates into the cells to replicate the mother's womb. The umbilical cord is the safety rope within the womb; outside the womb, the child's safety cord is the breath and the food. The breath is the cord between the soul and the Creator. And the food is the process of all growth, from a rice grain to a baby. This is known to all, yet experienced by few.

Anjali was born to a family that resided close to the banks of the legendary *kund*. A *kund* is a kind of tank or a water body constructed in days gone by to serve as a source of water. It is believed that this particular *kund* was visited by Lord Rama, Sita and Lakshmana during the 14 years they spent in exile. According to another legend, it is said that a devotee performed yogic prayers in the *kund* to meet the goddess of wealth. After 12 years of penance, the goddess finally appeared with pots of gold. Alas, by that time, the devotee had lost his lust for the yellow metal. The gold was buried around the *kund* and the goddess sent her guards to protect it. It is believed that the guards still stand around it, as the gods often visit this place. The *kund* is at the foot of a hill on which stands the temple of Lord Rama.

Anjali would often bathe in this *kund* and then meditate upon the waters, seeking answers to questions that were rooted in the depths of her subconscious.

She grew up in a loving family, yet she was often struck by the arrows of loneliness. Even though she was ignorant of the ways of the world, she would experience a lurking desire for something—a desire for something that seemed invisible, yet powerful. She was goaded by a mysterious search that seemed to have no reason. She spoke very little, as the depth of silence that lay within her seemed to be far less jarring than any communication with those around. Every sunset would cause her heart to bleed. This felt like an unsolvable mystery.

One day, while she was sitting meditatively at the *kund*, her sister, Sara, approached her. Concerned, she asked Anjali, "What is it that makes you so quiet?"

Anjali replied, "There is a quest that my heart knows but my mind cannot define. Until I know what this quest is, everything else seems futile. I cannot find any pleasure in things that make other people happy. I read about the Buddha and his great renunciation. While I am searching for the path, there seems to be something holding me back."

As she continued to look into the waters, she drew Sara's attention to their reflection. Anjali thoughtfully spoke, "Look carefully into the waters of the *kund*. I see you and myself in them, which seems as simple as that. Yet, I feel like I am chasing this reflection as a penance for something."

Sara was confused by her sister's words. "I do not understand," she said gently.

Even Anjali could not understand. Each time she saw a crease in the waters, she felt that she was born to learn something. Like the image the water reflected, she felt that her existence was not real. As the wind blew, there was a gentle ripple in the water. Anjali saw her image in the water, and with the ripple, her image quivered. This was her existence, fragile and unsubstantial.

She asked her sister, "What is it that I am born for? I know this existence is fragile. Yet I yearn for it. There is a void in my heart that I seek to fill. There is an emptiness that makes me sad when I look at the sunsets. There is a yearning, a hope, a dream to be happy. I sense that my birth opened my eyes to the world to go through the process of opening the third eye to the soul. This body is an instrument of realization. This body is an instrument to reach the destination, and the path is what I seek."

Then with a tinge of humour she revealed a mischievous thought, "The gods probably envy humans because of this body that allows the soul to experience all that is worldly. Men need the body to reach their Creator and, without the body, the Creator cannot enjoy his own creations."

The sisters laughed together. Their laughter brought a lightness to their conversation as well as a subtle revelation to Anjali, who felt a shiver run down her spine. With poised excitement, she declared to Sara, "Yes, I know what I yearn for. I yearn for love; love that is infinite, absolute and perfect. A love that will encompass my existence. A love that could give it substance and sustenance."

Sara wondered why Anjali yearned for the love she described when their mother already showered it upon them. "But Mother loves you the way you yearn for. No love would, or even could, fill the vacuum you feel in your heart more than your mother's love. The greatest meaning of love is that of a mother's for a child."

Anjali reflected upon this and said, "Yes, but one day, I will have to leave her or she will leave me. This awareness has filled my soul with pain. I realized this when I went out with my friends in the summers. The pain was so acute that I wept all the days that I was there. I missed her and I thought that I would die without her. I realized then that I may not always be with her, or she with me."

"But I can always be there with you!" Sara assured her.

"No, I know even you will have to leave someday. I search for a love that will be mine forever. One that will fill the void in my existence."

Sara sighed, "That may be a mirage."

Those words sounded familiar to Anjali. It reminded her of someone. It was a sacred feeling and as she sat, she could see his feet. Her soul shivered and echoed a verse from the distant springs of her being.

His lotus feet, so distant
A dream, now!
An awakening of the soul,
Mellowed by hushed sounds of longing, and cravings,
As emotions wreck internal space within.

And why did light pass into darkness?
For escape seems unreal,
Hardened by the winds of the mind;
And erring,
Wherein did soul repose faith?

Rebounding from distant echoes,
And saddening my heart,
Again, again, again, and again,
Did I cheat myself into all this?

Memories sit in the corners of my mind,
Playing, replaying their role,
As tides dig through shells of time.

Infinity lapses into a tremor,
Obscurity reduces to a naught,
Equilibrium reduces to a 'shunya'.

'Shunya' translates its rhythm into a wisp,
That crumples the castle of cards!

Buried memories stirred from the deep recesses of her mind and she felt an ache in her heart. She was aware somewhere in her subconscious that she had lost the privilege to serve those Lotus Feet—a privilege for which sages laboured. She knew that she had bargained for an endless, gnawing ache. An ache that lingered in her heart and compelled her to a quest that would not let her rest. This was the price she had paid for a faith she had lost. In its absence, she understood that life was painful and she, rudderless.

Anjali knew she had cheated herself and she was angry with herself. Anger led to frustration and frustration to a loss of discretion. Uncertain memories played lost themes and infinity seemed to collapse within the tremors of her soul. Her life appeared to be a castle of cards and the only redemption, she felt, would be the *shunya*, the void. Anjali felt miserable.

Sara glanced at what Anjali had written on the sand and watched it washed by the waters of the *kund*. She looked down at the *kund* once again. The *kund* was a mirror, reflecting all her hopes and desires and she began to recognize what Anjali had wanted her to see. She saw Anjali once again in the reflections of the still waters. She looked at Anjali and then at her reflection. Once again, she looked at her sister and saw her reflection in the waters. She could see the game of mirrors.

Between mirrors,
The possessor became the possessed;
Seen, the object.

Between mirrors,
The creator became the created,
Created, its creator.

A gentle breeze caressed the waters and Anjali watched her reflection merge with Sara's and there were no longer two reflections. Anjali was Sara and Sara was Anjali. Communion flowed, love strengthened. It was the game of mirrors.

Anjali knew that she stood on one side of the mirror and to see it differently, she would have to cross to the other. Yet, going to the other side was not easy. It would take a whole lifetime, maybe many. The game is complex. The game is played between the possessed and the possessor; between the created and the creator; between the object and the seer. Even though the opponent cannot be vanquished, he does give a fair chance because the Creator loves this game even more when his creation learns to play it well. He rejoices to see his creations master the game. For most, the illusion or *maya* cannot be conquered. However, there is a way around it.

That night, Anjali had a strange dream. She was sitting on a giant wheel whose radius stretched across several galaxies. As the wheel turned, it gained momentum, moving faster and faster. Anjali felt it move out of the earth's gravitational hold and knew that, very soon, she would be leaving the earth's orbit. Something within her made her afraid, when a voice outside asked, "Would you like to come to me?"

The voice asked again, "Would you like to come?"

Anjali took a hold of herself and said, "No! I want to return to earth." As she said this, she found herself back in the giant wheel, which began to slow down.

Anjali woke up with a rapidly beating heart. She was full of questions. Was it a dream? Did it really happen? For a long time, Anjali could not decide. Why was she afraid? Why had she opted not to be with Him? Was there a mission yet to be accomplished? A lesson yet to be learnt? For many years to come, the dream would haunt her and she would never know whether she had made the right choice.

A vibrant dawn appeared outside the window. She saw the young blossoms covered by dewdrops, awaiting the sun's rays. At twilight she saw the angels, all of whom she had known so well. She could hear them play invisible harps and the music lulled her heart. She continued to long for her unknown love, yet she knew in the depths of her being that it was a mirage. At night she looked at the sky filled with stars forming constellations and wondered if her quest lay somewhere distant in the skies.

Voila, the little prince laughs in his planet,
As my heart is torn by the last rays of the sun.

Innocence churns the sky,
Colours riot in pain and despair.

I go to stars where excellence is distilled in chambers of hope,
And, perfect awareness unsheathed swishes a sword;
Slicing love from life.

An art of living lost in the jungles of beauty,
Finds its roots in a breath.

All her thoughts invariably pointed to the truth; the truth about loving, the truth about living, the truth about her search.

As she experiences all that she has, Anjali was unaware that jealousy sowed the seeds of her desire to experience human love. Blinded by jealousy, she believed that love would own her exclusively and that she would own it alone. God had persuaded her not to take this journey but he knew the journey would free her from the pangs of jealousy and the bondages of desire as she travels through time and space.

chapter 4

Journey

The Master looked at Anjali but remained silent. She revealed to the Master that she was in search of perfect love. He then explained to her, "Like all of life, human love is self-limiting and so the desire for it should be conquered. Concentrate on the 'hara' and let the thinking start from there. 'Hara' is the wellspring of vital psychic energies. It is situated in the stomach. The centre of the universe is the pit of your belly."

Anjali found no comfort in his words. She decided to leave the monastery and return to the observatory. As she walked through the passageway of the monastery, she could hear young monks chanting as the bells tolled at harmonic intervals. She walked through the hamlet that housed the monastery and stopped at the edge, which overlooked the valley and the little town. The town reminded her of Shangri-La, the mystical, harmonious valley described in James Hilton's famous novel *Lost Horizon*. Anjali sat on the parapet and watched the horizon.

She observed her breath, which was hasty and intermittent, resonating the disturbance of her heart and soul. This was a contrast to the silence of the zen-like stillness around her. In an effort to calm her inner world, she whispered to herself, "This moment alone exists and yet, it is as transitory as the breath. Observe the breath and witness every inhalation and exhalation that brings a myriad of revelations as the mind is stilled."

She continued to direct herself into a meditation. As she meditated, she saw her ego repeatedly emerge in her thoughts in the form of desires. She traced her desires to their germination. She realized that her ego had slowly calcified over the years, taking a concrete shape and the desires had become increasingly compelling.

Deeper into the meditative state, Anjali felt as though the Master was seated in front of her, delivering a discourse: "As a child, your ego is malleable. Slowly, based on the shape given and the way you start interfacing with the world, you start becoming defensive and form structures and barriers that prevent elasticity to deal with the world objectively. This leads to self-centeredness, selfishness and competitiveness, all of which eventually create negativity that stunts growth into the spiritual space."

The Master slowly disappeared and only the essence remained. Anjali's visions became more distant and her pain less intense. When she gently opened her eyes, she experienced a certain level of stillness. In the sunset across the horizon, she could see the evening star rise. Night and day seemed to be battling. As she saw the last rays of the sun making the final exit, she lamented, "Alas! Another day sliced away from eternity." But once the exit was complete, the grief lost its sting and Anjali saw how masterly the stroke had been as numerous heavenly candles lit up the sky.

Questions steeped in wonderment floated in her mind— questions about the origin of the universe and the birth of time. "It all seems like an illusion. Nothing was created, nor did it exist, nor ever was, neither will ever be. Yet, my emotions are so real and so painful," she acknowledged thoughtfully.

She felt time and space curl on itself and embrace each other. As she floated in her imagination, Anjali was moving on the Mobius strip, one with her breath, unaware of time and space.

When she woke up from her trance, it was past 10 pm. Four hours had slipped away in what seemed like minutes.

She hurried to the bus stop but the last bus had already left. She decided to walk back to the observatory, where she was studying the stellar events.

Anjali asked a tribal for directions. He knew the word "observatory" and showed her the way. But after walking a while, she could not recall the directions. She smiled to herself as she remembered how her friends would sarcastically call her "the world's finest navigator" as she often confused the simplest of maps and would reach nowhere. She almost always missed a turn and ended up where she started.

It was nearing midnight and Anjali had still not reached the observatory. Suddenly, another tribal emerged from behind the trees. He looked at her quizzically, and she responded matter-of-factly, "Observatory."

The observatory was a prominent feature of that area as scientists, scholars and students from all over the world came to study the interstellar phenomena and the solar flares. It was located 25 km from the township, on a relatively higher altitude where the winds are strong. Apart from a few telescopes and other equipment, the observatory had remained untouched by humans.

The tribal smiled as he led her through a patch of dense forest of the Nilgiri Hills. They reached the end of the boundary of a tribe to find the beginning of another. At this point, as if from nowhere, yet another tribal stepped out from behind a tree. The tribal who had led Anjali thus far signalled her to go along with the next tribal.

Just as she was to restart her journey with the new tribesman, she looked at her watch. It was well past midnight. This tribal led her to the next, where another tribal took charge of her. She crossed six tribal territories like that. She was amazed by the change of charge as each tribesman led her to the next person awaiting her. While walking through the sixth tribal zone, she thought to herself, "The message seems to be transmitted from one territory to the next, as if through an invisible wire or an inaudible voice whispering through an invisible corridor of time."

At a distance, Anjali could see a small light flickering along with the faint sound of the drums. She gestured to the tribal that she would like to go and rest there for a while before traveling further. The tribal pointed to the other direction and said the word "observatory". Through sign language, she communicated to the tribesman that she was tired and hungry.

He took her through the forest, towards the light. The sound of the drums got louder and louder as she approached a huge fire, around which tribal men and women were dancing to perfect rhythm. Their steps were vigorous and enthusiastic. Anjali loved the sight. Seeing them, she recalled her guru's words, "Life is a celebration. You must celebrate every minute of it." She now knew what her guru meant.

Watching the tribals dance, she bemoaned, "Life is a celebration for these tribals who live amid nature. They value the essence of life and living. Why can't I be like them? Why is it so difficult for me to celebrate the moment instead of yearning for something unknown? If only my search could end. If only my desire could be fulfilled. If only it could evaporate. Then, surely, I will be able to celebrate life."

As Anjali sat in front of the fire, something strange occurred. The dazzle of the fire projected colours in which she could see shapes and forms dance in abstraction.

Anjali mused:

Into a journey inward,
I breathe the fresh air of hills.

Rhythms are restored,
From patterns emerges a god who speaks.

Beauties rush,
Escalating into a deafening sound are echoes of silence.
With each returning,
I remember, history repeats itself,
Through resurrection, and transmigration, life restored.

In ethereal calm,
Unsung songs are heard.
In far cries, sounds of spring,
In songs, his voice.
The voice is silent and distant,
Now louder,
With each moment louder and louder.
Before it, I see a spectacle,
A spectacle in which his creation bows to him

The tribals brought her some boiled grass and seeds to eat. The simple food filled her stomach as the flames of the fire seemed to fill her soul. She closed her eyes and slipped into a deep slumber.

chapter 5

Apparition

Streets are arched with branches from ruins that line streets.
The birds twitter in barren trees,
Looking for a shade to build a nest.

A corpse rises from a grave,
It walks in grace.
Its steps are full of weighty ease,
And wonder fills corridors,
As the corpse walks in hollow streets of time!

Autumn has come so suddenly,
And only winter lies in front.
The corpse looks up to the sky,
Looking for shade.
It nods its head,
Alas! Only to find searching souls,
And continues its walk in hollow streets of time.

The air is silent,
As an uneasy stillness
Fills the space.
Death, desolation, isolation form a ring around the corpse,
As it stands at crossroads.

As if dismissing all,
It furrows its way through the hollow streets of time.

An unearthly apparition takes to sword
And summoning its allies, attacks.
The corpse stands unhurt
Shielded by death!
The corpse cannot live to die,
Nor breathe.
No dreams fill its heart,
Lifeless as a stone,
And beckoning much,
It walks the hollow streets of time.

Forsaken by a past,
Unanticipated by a future,
Non-existent now,
The corpse looks around,
Unloved, uncared,
Invisible to a world.
The corpse stands at ease,
Attending all,
Mourning the deceased
It walks the hollow streets of time.

Memories pounce at him,
For, he was once a child,
And now
Forgotten,
Misunderstood, mislaid, misplaced and dislocated.
A fractured heart he carries now,
Through hollow streets of time!

All waters swim to sea,
Limped pools fill his eyes.
In the blue,
It sees a vision,
Dear and unknown,
And a horizon lost,
Through the hollow streets of time!

With dusk and dawn,
The corpse stands in a twilight zone.
Vision escapes a sigh,
And future adjacent to the dead,
Lies in pain, intractably, in disdain,
Looking into the hollow streets of time!

Eternity takes a resort,
Condemned thus,
The corpse finds a respite in echoed despair.
It lifts its head,
And walks above the ground,
An inch above metallic roads,
It sets its course,
Through the hollow streets of time.

Anjali looked at the corpse and questioned it, "Who are you?"

The corpse replied, "I am the fate of mankind."

Bewildered, Anjali said, "Oh, can mankind not escape you?"

The corpse replied, "I seek my redemption. I seek to overcome *my* fate but alas, I am condemned to walk in the hollow streets of time."

Anjali felt sad for the corpse; for the fate of every human. She remembered that she was human too now and worriedly asked the corpse, "Who has condemned you thus? Why does it seem like you walk through the hollow streets of time?"

The corpse replied, "Mankind has destroyed the essence of time and made it hollow. I was a king a long time ago when mankind was sane. At that time, I wore robes lined with rare gems and my crown was made of gold. I walked in grandeur, the universe was at my command. I owed it all to him, because only he was my master. I bowed to him day and night. This was a long time ago, when mankind knew how to use time. Now I am condemned."

Anjali enquired again, this time with more compassion, "Who has condemned you?"

In response, the corpse asked her, "Do you know what has divested time of its power? Do you know what has made time hollow?"

Anjali replied, "Time is mightier than any other creation. Time is not hollow."

The corpse insisted, "For me it is hollow. Do you know why it is hollow according to me?"

Anjali thought for a while and answered, "Desire and longing, or possibly a foolish unknown search is what makes time hollow. I have experienced this too. Instead of celebrating life and thanking God for every moment of existence, my search for an unknown prince causes me immense pain. This longing makes time hollow for me."

The corpse explained, "Like you, everyone is in search of something. Mankind is an unsatisfied breed. Time is an endless stream of precious gems that you have to polish and use appropriately. Only then does life become a worthwhile celebration. Do you know that each minute is more precious than the jewels in a crown? Humans spend hours admiring the jewels of a crown little knowing that life offers them treasures more precious. They treat time as dust and let it blow away into oblivion. Sometimes humans consider time to be as annoying as insects and kill it. There are humans who treat time as a prostitute, using it to fulfil their wanton desires."

Anjali probed further, "How can I add value to my time? How can I polish it and use it purposefully so that the jewels glitter brightly?"

The corpse responded, "Only by seeking the real. The unreal does not exist, and the real never ceases to be. Your unknown desire and your unknown prince do not exist. The One, and the only one who exists, is the only reality. Live in this realization and your life will be full of purpose. Time will then be at your command and your fate will not be like mine."

Anjali felt a stabbing pain in her heart when she heard this. She experienced a strong resistance to give up her desire for her prince. She could not let go of her search. She was confident that her unknown prince existed, even if he was on the other side of the world or maybe on the other side of the universe. She was sure one day she would find him and experience perfect love. She was prepared to take birth repeatedly in varied forms, on different planets, across galaxies. She knew that she would find him at some point in her existence.

Anjali woke up from her dream feeling tormented yet hopeful. The tribals continued to dance, the fire was still ablaze. The sound of the drums could be heard in the background. It was 3.30 am; she had slept for almost two hours. The tribal who had brought her there was sitting next to her, patiently waiting for her to stir from her slumber. Anjali looked at him and wondered, "Why does he effortlessly feel responsible for my comfort and safety? In stark contrast, I tend to shoulder my responsibilities with impatience and the burden of efforts. Maybe it is because I am not his burden. I am his responsibility."

Filled with admiration, Anjali gushed to herself, "This man is practicing Zen, unadulterated by the consciousness of it. I wish I could be like him someday."

She snapped out of her thoughts and signalled to him that she wanted to restart their journey to the observatory. The tribal got up enthusiastically and led the way till they reached the end of his territory. He pointed to the paved road that would lead her to the observatory. She turned to thank him but before she could say anything, he was on his way back to his tribesmen. Watching him disappear into the dense forest, she thought, "Only innocence and simplicity can call for such humility. He did not even need a gesture of gratitude to know he has done a good deed. He is probably filled with immense faith, a faith in life, faith in the self, and above all faith in the power that makes all this happen." She bowed in reverence towards his direction, then turned towards her path to the observatory.

chapter 6

Fantasy

Dawn was painting its beautiful colours in the sky as Anjali neared the observatory. There was nobody in sight. She sat on a rock, at the edge of the hill, to relax for a while before she could take on the day.

Even though she was tired, her conscious mind became aware of images being projected from her subconscious. She observed, in awe, the vibrant colours of dawn welcoming the morning rays, while the moon still shone bright in the sky.

Against her half-closed eyes, a vivid vision appeared.

A glass mountain,
Angels descending on dew drops,
Dancing with the first rays of sunshine.

The dawn becoming brighter,
As night unites with the day.
The day taking shape,
In colours of the morning.

The glens with imps and devilkin,
The valleys of death,
And yet in it, crucibles of life.
Treasures lying in ocean depths,
And a pearl taking shape.

Anjali knew that all this was real.

The glass mountain suddenly disappeared, and with it the angels, the imps and the devilkins. Anjali understood that the communication that had been briefly established had suddenly delinked. She looked at the morning sky, which seemed to reveal to her:

A parallax of vision,
A communication discontinues,
A skewness of thoughts,
And astigmatism blinds perception!

Words as symbols,
Refuse to communicate.
All senses jarred,
A link breaks!

That was not true. The link had given her a glimpse, if only briefly, of another world. Anjali knew that this was:

A world across the rainbow;
A land of silence,
Where senses do not work,
The eye only inwardly perceives,
Lips break into a candid smile.
On this land only the soul of man is known.

She heard a voice sing to her:

Sugar and plum,
The candy is within.
'I' at the centre,
The eye cannot see.

Glasses behind the bushes,
The crystal cave disappears.
A soul pawned,
Is ambushed.

Anjali shouted back at the voice:

Frighten the maundering bigots,
To a point of delight.
Where in carved rhythms,
Music would yawn and escape.
Revelling in complacency,
Eternity would still outlive seconds,
And in it, the 'I' shall disappear!

The voice retorted:

Yet minutes replaced would still slice time,
And the 'I' shall never disappear completely.

A gentle breeze and she heard another voice speak:

In rhythms, life accentuates and evolves,
Neutralized by suffering, pain dissolves!
With it, the 'I' dissolves.

From ruins, temples are reclaimed,
Sanctum-sanctoriums radiate that magic charm,
In which the soul shall reign.

The first disdainful voice asserted:

Alas! Scattered bits have pawned the soul to Satan,
For there is no hope,
As the temple cannot be reclaimed again.

Anjali had been a brilliant student, accomplishing much academically. But none of her accomplishments meant anything to her on this day. She felt insecure and incomplete, a huge void filled her heart. Something was missing.

Filled with distress, she addressed the second voice, hoping it would pacify her:

Could accomplishments come to my rescue?
Or could simplicity resume its feet?
The lustre has died,
And insecure profanity ceases to please.

The second voice gently assured her:

Fear not, O mortal divine!
For crossing swords, you have crossed the minds,
Overcoming quandaries of battleships.
You can build a life divine,
By striking a wonder,
Struck with time.

Anjali confidently promised herself:

I shall seal the pain in my heart,
I shall instruct my mind to trace each breath.
In every attempt I shall scan the world within,
Till emotions,
That travel like satellites around 'I,'
Disintegrate.
And, there then emerges a non-self,
To make God in the temple smile.

As Anjali said these words, she saw the glass mountain appear again. In it, she saw the Master. He was talking to the prince she had seen from the skies. As she longingly wished she was an angel with wings, the rays of the rising sun melted the glass mountain of her vision.

chapter 7

Perception

When everyone at the observatory saw Anjali, they were relieved that she had returned safe and sound. All hailed her as the 'Queen of the Forests' when she narrated her adventures of the night to them.

The experiments at the observatory continued as usual but her memory was clouded by the visit to the monastery, her return journey through the night and the various visions she had had. She felt compelled to visit the monastery every day and sit on the hill and meditate. Fortunately, she never missed the last bus back again.

One day, when visiting the monastery, she revealed to the Master, "The other day, I had a vision of you in a glass mountain. You were talking to the same prince whose love is my mission."

With a gentle smile, the Master said to her, "If you want to pursue your path of realization, you will have to walk through fire. Walking in love is like walking through fire. You know what fire does?"

Anjali replied, "Fire reduces the combustible to ashes."

"Yes, and fire also turns metal into pure gold. You must walk through fire," the Master revealed.

Anjali prayed to the Master to grant her this wish.

The Master assured her, "I will grant you your wish," but warned her, "But not for the taste of pleasure."

That evening when Anjali returned to the observatory, she experienced pangs of sadness. Her studies at the observatory were coming to an end.

With only a few days remaining, she pursued her studies with a zeal she had not known before. She looked at the stars more intently and studied the solar flares and the stellar phenomena with a steadfastness that her friends had not witnessed before. Her longing was fading. Her mind was in control, getting disciplined by the rigours of science. She began to wonder whether her mission was indeed to learn about love.

While looking into the sky on her last night at the observatory, she observed in wonderment, "The universe is vast and yet there is a certain unity in it. This unity whispers through the layers of time and space, echoing repeatedly, 'All is ONE.' Past, present, future collapse into One, as infinity collapses into a point. Beyond this point, there are many, many points, and many more infinities. This is where nothing exists and yet the One is." This realization made her shiver with an excitement she had never experienced.

She felt lighter as she considered the magnanimity of the present moment. Every cell of her being celebrated. She experienced herself being present in the now.

She sat that night intently observing the patterns that adorned the night sky. She felt the planets reveal their individual personalities to her, and their effect on human lives. She learnt far more that night than she did during her entire stay at the observatory. This was not a night of knowledge but of wisdom that the universe gifted her.

A questioning poem flowed through her mind as she gazed at the stars.

A beat is pulsating,
A tune in obeisance asks thy surveillance.
The soprano crescendos, asks:
Will thou care?
I wait.

To give, I must get from thee
What I must give to come back again to life?
Must I take to alms and lie low?
Or, must I asking alms for arms,
Bid farewell to both?

To create from nothing that something,
And to dissolve this something,
Into nothing,
Life's mission would be accomplished!

She knew she needed to surrender all her desires and missions to God's will. A surrender in which she should dissolve herself. A surrender in which she should dissolve the unreal and therefore the non-existent.

She knew all this intellectually, yet she was unable to surrender. She reminded herself of the Master's words, "The world is an illusion, and more so the emotions. Observe the emotions dispassionately. Let them not steer you as you sit in stillness." However, she was aware that she was driven by the stormy winds of her emotions. She was entirely under their spell.

She closed her eyes and saw the vision of twilight cast upon the canvas of her imagination.

I see sunshine drops slowly fill the time glass.
I hear voices in echoes of a whisper.

I see my prayers light an ember, as inspirations daunt and dare!
I look into and beyond the horizons at a dream lost,
I see into the horizon, mirages disappear.

Into the horizon,
A sunset,
A silence sliced!

Into the horizon,
A vision located
A bond with life.

Into the horizon,
A pain passes in vain.

Into the horizon,
Two shadows sail in front of me,
As moon paces across the sky,
As stars stud the night.

I remember the palm trees that line the shore,
The sun reflected from windows,
And coconut fronds high on the doors.

Into the horizon,
Two shadows walk in front of me,
A child in their arms,
A farewell note in background,
A vision links past with now.
For, my home is beyond.

I see the unreal take hold of the real,
I see the unreal daunt the real.

Into the horizon,
Steps that echoed on the road haunt me,
As I see once again two shadows walk in front of me,
This time, no one walks with them.

Into the horizon,
Sunset is far behind,
The moon has not risen yet.

Into the horizon,
I hear deafening stillness capture every sound,
Of frosted beats of a broken heart,
Slicing silence into two.

The haunting stillness does not stop the rotation of earth,
As sun and life pulsates at its core.

She experienced the circle of life and witnessed the drama that stages day and night, union and separation, birth and death—in episodes as per the script. She observed the movement of time, its mystery, its journey and its reversal.

In stilled ether, I see hope rebuild a harbour in it,
As I see myself anchored in a time glass.
I see a miracle occur,
Sunshine drops evaporate,
Reversing time.

Anjali reminded herself, "Redemption happens only with the realization that all is an illusion, including time and emotions."

Into the horizon,
This time I see a shadow walk in front of me,
I see myself walk in it,
As I see shadows walk behind.
I see now the evening star,
And no shadow walks thereafter!

It was now time for her to leave the observatory. As she packed her belongings she resolved, "I must visit the monastery to seek blessings from the Master before embarking on my homeward journey." A shiver ran up her spine with the imminent departure from the town.

chapter 8

Metamorphosis

Anjali woke up just before daybreak. She was inspired by the colours cast upon the horizon as she witnessed the first rays of sunshine dissolve the morning dew.

And in this motion of time,
A rhythm pulsates through the universe
Nature ever so empowered,
As winds play with virgin gold.

The senses purified,
Dreams enshrine in some sacred space,
All infatuation melts into the serenity of surrender.

She felt liberated. Liberated from all bondage. Liberated from dreams. For long enough, she had indulged herself in desires that were profane. In the beauty of nature, she recognized that all those dreams hold little or no value at all.

She saw the life of Buddha more clearly than ever before.

Rooted in compassion,
On a razor's edge,
His life wed to eternity.

The bells toll,
And chords invisible strike a note.

Anjali reached the monastery and bowed before the Buddha. He was unmoved and untouched, his smile as candid as ever. His body strong, his mind made of stainless steel, his heart an endless ocean of love. The early morning sunlight cast a divine spell on the bronze sculpture. Anjali sat in the lotus pose and meditated upon her breath. She was surprised that her breathing was not calm and steady, fluttering instead like a butterfly emerging from the cocoon for the first time.

She heard her inner voice explain, "Just as the caterpillar metamorphoses into the butterfly, so also after travelling through a long dark tunnel—from the end of which a stream of light enters—you are welcomed to a different reality. Break free from the past and leap into the future to complete this journey. Nonetheless, it will ache when you leave the past behind, an ache that blends with excitement as you come face to face with your destiny."

The calm inner voice continued, "All this is temporary. All that you experience shall pass, and so your present state of being is irrelevant." Anjali suddenly regained equanimity. She delved deeper into her meditation, observing the sensations of every part of her body. Her inner voice repeated the word, *"Anitya! Anitya! Anitya!"* This made her experience a stillness.

She had first learnt about the concept of *anitya* from the Master, who had explained to her, *"Anitya* is the eternal impermanence of everything. When your heart flutters in anxiety, or fear clouds your composure, remind yourself of this word that represents the eternal impermanence and observe stillness dissolve all unrest."

After a while, Anjali stirred out of her meditation and cast her eyes upon the statue of Buddha. He was smiling at her. She sat there, looking at the beautifully sculptured idol, wondering, "What is the significance of the smile I see? Is he trying to tell me something?"

Then her contemplative mind shifted towards the monks, "How must their families feel about them choosing the ascetic way of life? How did they bid farewell to each other? Are their mothers in agony or ecstasy knowing their sons are on the divine path and will never return home? What could have drawn these young monks to asceticism? Was it a call of the divine, or an urge to make their families proud, or an escape from the stress of daily living? Or, was it that their families had sent them thus? Were they bound by duty to the 'law' to become monks?"

A monk pulled her out of her ponderings. "The Master is ready to see you in his quarters. You will not be able to see him in private as he is with a visitor." Anjali was disappointed because she had been eager to get a few minutes alone with the Master. She knew nothing could be done and walked along with the monk to the Master's quarters.

As she entered the doorway of the Master's meeting room, she saw the visitor's back. She walked straight to the Master to seek his blessings. The Master gestured to her to sit across from him, next to the visitor. She took her seat and felt her breath pick up an erratic pace. As she turned towards her visitor, she went numb. She felt herself freeze and dissolve into a timeless eternity, her soul never to be reclaimed again.

Her prince was the visitor seated next to her.

She heard her inner voice exclaim, "Your vision of your prince talking to the Master in the glass mountain was not an illusion!" She asked her inner voice, "Is the Master responsible for this encounter with my prince? Or has this been ordained by the planets and constellations?"

The Master turned towards Anjali and said, "The journey has just begun. Go in peace, but remember you must pass through fire before you become pure gold. Strengthen yourself because there is much to suffer in the future. Live in dharma and to its perfection. You must celebrate pain too. Observe your breath as a *drishta*, the dispassionate observer, with equanimity."

For the first time Anjali felt she could not share her feelings with the Master. Her mind asked her inner voice, "What would the Master think of me if I told him the visitor sitting next to me is my prince?" Looking at the visitor, she felt dejected. The prince did not seem to return her excitement and was cool about her presence. She sat there for a long time, feeling his presence. She wanted to speak to him, however, she felt that it was inappropriate to do so. The cacophony of sounds of her chattering mind muffled her wise inner voice. After waiting for a considerable time, she could hear her ego commanding her, "It is time to leave." She silently got up and bowed in front of the Master for his blessings. He flashed an enigmatic smile at her as she turned to leave, in silence, disappointed and helpless.

Anjali sat outside the monastery, hoping her prince would come there and meet her. But he did not. Nevertheless, she was confident her true love would be reciprocated. She waited for hours, but he did not emerge from the monastery. Every moment of waiting stretched into eternity. Dejected, she told herself, "Now that I have seen my prince, it will be painful to endure his absence."

A surge of doubt engulfed her. "What if I never meet him again? What if he is oblivious of my presence? After all, it is I who yearned for him from heaven. It is I who have desired him. What if he does not reciprocate my love? Why should he?" She experienced the stabbing ache of unreciprocated love and questioned herself in agony, "Is it really true?" Then she reminded herself, "I have longed for him. I have dreamed about him. He is my mission."

She assured herself, "Meeting my prince could not be a coincidence. Nothing in life is a coincidence. There is a master plan and everything fits perfectly well, one into the other."

She then experienced stillness; she remembered the Master say, "Once the vision is reversed in time, everything falls into place. The trick is to live backwards in time and, if that is not possible, the perspective can be confirmed only when the eyes can refocus and look from the other side of the time glass. This is not easy. This can be done by sharpening your alertness. The sharpened alertness has to be pointed. To achieve this, you have to master the art of controlling your confusing mind, judgmental intellect and discriminating ego, which can only be achieved by non-attached attachment."

As the momentary stillness faded away, the chattering of her mind began to disturb her again, "I do not know what the future has in store for me. I do not know how I will meet my prince again. He is just a few meters away, though it feels like galaxies exist between us."

She glanced at the monastery one last time before heading to the bus stop.

As she walked, she felt as though her peace was shattered and equanimity destroyed. She realized, "Peace is brittle, and equanimity is ever so fragile."

Once seated on the bus, her mind wandered back to the prince. "It feels like peace had never reached my soul. It was only on the surface. Equanimity is a long and arduous practice. I have a long way to go. I reach a state of equanimity only when provocation is missing. I have been tricked. My jealous

God must be smiling. My heart has overtaken my peace and ruined it."

In agony she wondered, "Do I lack faith? Is the prince actually my mission?"

The day passed painfully and, with the sunset, the agony only intensified. She implored:

Cloaked in a blanket of night,
Betrayed by my own faith,
Or lack of it,
O God, I seek thy grace.

Stifled by my own convictions,
And its refusal of love,
O Lord, I await thy sign.

Consistently at a loss of meaning,
Of joy, of beauty,
O Master, I pray to thee.

Carried by fate,
I seek life,
O Divine, but not this way.

O Father!
Must I stay?
Must the heart ache till throbs of time cease their beat?
Or must it bleed,
With blows of destiny,
To endure tears,
And, all pain that goes with it!

My God!
Must I kiss these storms?
Storms that wreck my soul,
Storms that do not retreat,
Storms that are muted by symphonies,
Storms that revel in tears of human hearts,
And, all pain that goes with it!

O!
How those cellular academics,
The intellectual facade,
Like shadows prevented a view.

How it mixed solace with blues?
Never striking roots,
And false equanimity,
Glazed waters with unreal hues.

Do I purge myself in wars within?
In tears of the human heart,
And all pain that goes through it?

O God!
How I love to endear to human love,
And in it find an end to my journey.

How with lightning that struck my heart,
With cupid's arrows,
I saw light!

In light much damage was done,
In noise many echoes heard.

With a fear of loss,
In hesitant steps, I took to insist,
And in insistence,
I lost a touch of class.

All beauties and joys led to tears of the human heart,
And all pain that goes with it!

She tried to get a grip over herself and reassert her mind over her heart. She clenched her hands in prayer, pleaded with her own self to be still, and pledged to herself a silence not yet practiced. She prayed for stillness because...

It alone, in its vibrancy could manifest,
That which was positive, pure,
That stillness!
That in precious submission to his will,
Would reclaim humility and stillness,
That through surrender would find,
That path through the golden gate.

A gate, which in silence leads to faith.
And to a journey through tears,
That drowns the human heart,
And all pain that goes with it.

She knew all this was imperfect but understood that in imperfections she must find the perfect.

Through his acceptance,
His grace would come.

Not through words,
But only when the heart surrenders,
In silence and in tears,
And with all the pain that goes with it.

The pain was mounting upon her heart, and she felt her heart would break under its weight.

I have reached the end of a road;
A dead end, a cul-de-sac!

"Will I ever reach my destination? Or will I be led into disenchantment. What is this journey? Is it a journey into nothingness? Or one that leads into an endless pain that lingers on, birth after birth, haunting the human heart? I know desires lead to suffering. In fact, desires are the root and possibly the only cause of suffering," she contemplated. She foresaw great suffering...

As hope crumbles,
And disillusionment is total,
Pain heads to a cul-de-sac!

She tried to ease the pain that struck her heart but to no avail. The moving bus seemed to rock her, making her eyes heavy. She rested her head and felt someone gently soothe her to sleep.

chapter 9

Time

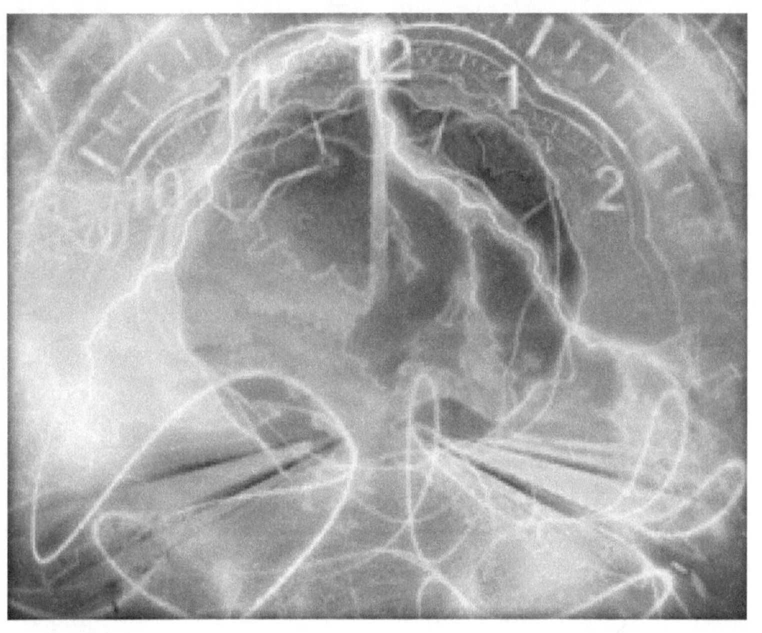

Anjali's mother and sister were extremely happy to have her back home. She showed them the studies she had conducted at the observatory and told them about the monastery and the Master. Despite all her excitement, her mother and sister noticed a sadness in her eyes. They wondered why she seemed so sad, but they did not want to upset her, so they did not enquire.

One day, while sitting at the *kund* with her sister, Anjali confessed:

I saw a strange dream,
Brief, silent, intense, significant.
It never recurred,
Yet, every day of my remaining life I shall live it.
Hoping it never happens,
Longing for it to come true,
Too afraid that it may,
Dying for it to come to pass,
Living every moment in the hope,
It never does.

Anjali asked Sara, "What is the purpose of the drops of water in this *kund*?"

Sara replied, "Must everything have a purpose?"

"Yes, everything must have a purpose. I wonder, what could be the purpose of these drops in this *kund*?"

Sara said thoughtfully, "The purpose of these drops is to evaporate. They must evaporate to keep the circle of life going. They must evaporate to return as raindrops that fill up the *kund*."

Anjali responded, "That means their purpose is to lose their identity. But how could that be their purpose? I feel the purpose of these water drops is to find their way into an oyster shell and become a pearl. Only those drops get fulfilment that become pearls. From nothing, they become something priceless."

Sara refuted Anjali's claim. "That is untrue because a drop of water is truly priceless, whereas a pearl has a price. Life cannot sustain itself without water. Water is life, therefore priceless. A pearl is beautiful and rare but it does not sustain life. The essential is always ordinary and freely available and that is the miracle."

Anjali appreciated her sister's point of view. "That is a wonderful way of looking at things. But why do we always try to look towards making our lives purposeful when the real purpose of life is life itself? Maybe the real purpose is to lose our identity?"

Sara pondered, "The problem with you, Anjali, is that you want to be different. You want to be extraordinary. The truth is that it is far more difficult to be ordinary and simple. For you, Anjali, it is important that you be ordinary. Always remember, the essential is ordinary."

The two sisters enjoyed such discussions that enriched each other with their varying perspectives. Anjali looked up to Sara as a mentor, as she felt her sister was far more evolved. She could trust Sara to provide her with the path to meaningful insights.

During her studies, Anjali had been often wonderstruck by the mystery of time.

Once, while sitting with the Master at the monastery, she had asked him about the power of time. What he said left a deep impression on her mind and made her see time as a formless form. The Master had explained, "Time *is*, as timeless and time go together. If time ends then nothing remains. It is the ultimate dimension. It can pave ways. It goes on microscopically. In many ways, time is a paradox in itself and yet the ultimate reality."

She had sat awestruck, listening to the Master as he continued, "Nobody has been able to measure time, all the so-called measures are metaphors created by the Masters through time. Yet, nobody knows how it is sequenced and in what way it can be lured. You are in a kind of stream of time in which sudden upheavals and sudden islands of peace and silence can come. What cannot be foreseen is time."

Recalling the Master's description of time, Anjali thought to herself, "Time is an enigmatic force that has a creator like everyone else. Time rules the world. It makes nations powerful and reduces civilizations to naught. It reins hopes and builds characters. It turns paupers into kings and returns blossoms to dust. It reduces rocks to ash. It dominates the entire creation and every creature born or unborn bows to it."

As the thoughts began to flow, she wrote in her journal, "Time moves in discrete packets. Each quantum has a separate existence and unique personality. Each personality is cast depending on the time of its birth and the influence of the stars and their configurations at that time. But if time determines the constellations and the stars, how could these constellations and stars determine time's own destiny? At this point, logic would inevitably fail and poetry would start."

She decided to indulge her sister with her thoughts while they sat at the *kund* one evening. She nudged Sara, "Let us assume that time shaped space and the dimensions." After a brief pause, pleased that she had captured her sister's attention, Anjali went on to explain, "Then there must be another dimension, which would govern time. Maybe this dimension could be an unreality, or maybe a higher reality beyond human comprehension."

Sara urged her to continue. With a gentle smile, Anjali continued, "Time exists in different layers, in different dimensions, each layer created differently, governed differently, existing in curvatures, existing simultaneously, formed into eternity, and maybe this eternity moves into yet another dimension, into the harmony of existence, the harmony of a master plan."

After pausing to take a few deep breaths, Anjali revealed to Sara, "Time is a parallel of Shiva. It creates and destroys within a moment. It is birth and death, union and separation, war and peace, all happening simultaneously. What is happening now has happened in another dimension of space, for time and space are two sides of the same coin. There are various aspects interfacing with each other within which time, space and energy are all layers."

Sara looked at Anjali with pride as they spent the rest of the evening in awe of the magnanimity of time.

The debates would thus go on and on...

One day at sunset, as Anjali sat at the edge of the *kund*, she observed the ripples and their movement with time. She saw faces appear in the water. They seemed like real faces; real persons with unreal features. Each one looked like a soldier, wearing a distinct uniform that represented different battalions.

When Anjali looked at them closely, they were not soldiers but persons wearing different colours and styles. Their features were constantly changing. Sometimes they appeared young and frivolous, sometimes grave and serious, sometimes wise and godly. "This seems like the march of time. The march of a different dimension. The march of personalities that carry in them the power of history," she thought to herself, immersed in the state of wonderment created by the vision.

Anjali bowed and addressed the battalions of time:

O! Wise soldiers of time,
Guarding battles of life,
O! Mighty crew,
Sailing on a rainbow,
In empty ships,
And battle ships.
Do you wage a war?
Or redeeming all,
Purge sin?

Anjali looked at the soldiers more intently and realized that every soldier moving beyond the periphery of her vision would end up falling into oblivion.

She thought, "They are entering into another dimension of reality; possibly through a black hole into another universe or into another dimension of time. They do not die when they go out of sight."

Her mind was inundated with a thousand questions. "Are these soldiers immortal? Do they continue their journey from one time dimension to another, and yet another, endlessly? Do they have a final destination? Is their destination unto God?"

Anjali began to comprehend that, "Every moment that is here and now lives in its relative existence. It undoubtedly continues its journey onwards into new spaces and new time horizons. It curls again, and again, maybe infinitely. So, maybe at times, it even falls back into horizons it has crossed before. Is it because of this we sometimes see past events repeat, ghosts reappear, or history occurring in front of us?"

Anjali attempted to speak to them again:

In silence and fury,
Yet unchanging,
You ride a wave,
Changing all,
Rewarding brave,
You, yourself changeless.

As her mind was silenced, she heard a soldier reveal to her:

Tearing sunshine,
We march in battalions,
Through graveyards,
And grape wines,
Through changing landscape
We overflow,
And outlive lifetimes.

Impudently questioning hope,
Impudently determining a course,
Unveiling slowly,
Untying the Gordian knot,
We walk in grace,
We follow grace.

Deluding illusions,
Dismantling dogmas,
Reasserting faith,
Measure-to-measure,
Without haste,
We march at a measured pace.

Always looking into his face,
Chasing his pace,
Our steps do not falter,
Our crew does not race,
Our sergeants unlike mortal leaders never die,
No waste ever lies.

In proportion,
In perfection,
Inch-by-inch, and eternally,
In untiring revelation,
And paternally, we foster humankind.
We plead with humankind,
To learn,
To love,
To know,
His candid steps
His mysterious smile.

Anjali understood that she had heard something that maybe none else could ever hope to hear. "Maybe it is a brief spell of inspiration when the senses are suddenly sharpened and the inward eye opens to reveal a rare phenomenon. Maybe the great sages have passed through similar moments of inspiration. Possibly, what made them sages was not passing through these moments of inspiration but their capacity to stay in such moments of inspiration. For only they could live in the past, the present and the future simultaneously. Only they could be immune to the swings of destiny. In fact, since they conquered the relativity of time and space, they could even travel backwards in time. This is possible only because the great sages conquered the heart of the Creator and that was not easy," she told herself, admiring every sage of spiritual greatness.

In adoration, she addressed the soldiers:

O! Brave soldiers of time,
Empowered by him,
To rule,
You rule humankind.

"Even though each one of them is immortal, yet each one of them is impermanent in the here and now. Nothing and no one could be permanent. This is the divine illusion."

Anjali observed her breath with dispassion, becoming aware of the pain and torment she was experiencing deep within her being. She knew that all this was impermanent but the weight of it was so heavy that it felt unbearable. She held her breath, as if to stall the movement of time, as the soldiers marched on.

The Message

One day while sitting by the *kund*, Anjali recalled the words of the Master, "I will grant you your wish but not for the taste of pleasure."

She thought to herself, "I will someday meet my prince, but what did the Master mean when he had said, I will grant you your wish but not for the taste of pleasure?"

Several days after she had returned home, Anjali wrote to the Master about her vision of the glass mountain and the feelings she had experienced when she saw the 'guest' at his cottage on the last day.

The Master wrote back instructing her to watch her breath.

Anjali wrote back:

"Passions knit a web,
As love daunts a thread,
Maddening blindness lures a vision,
Obsessed and confused,
I rebel.

Yet threads weave a garland,
In it streams of thoughts flow,

In it, dust in sunshine glows,
In it diamonds line a hope.

A robe is woven,
A path ordained for me to move,
In quiet melody,
In flow of nature,
Up stairways,
Up horizons,
With every breath begins an awareness,
Into an ocean of oneness,
Streams chill winds of change.

An ego gathers dust,
With it, it assumes a shape, a size,
An ego searching blossoms makes mistakes.

The Master replied:

An ego, crying redemption, shatters,
The origin of universe in its melody echoes,
Aum.

The Master's words gave little solace as she waited, tempting her fate.

One day by the *kund,* as Anjali wondered about the march of time, she noticed a dove and watched it absent-mindedly for a long time. She realized the dove was not afraid of her, as it came closer and closer. She saw that it carried a message tied to its legs.

She took it in her hand and untied the message, which read, "You looked good at the Master's cottage."

The prince had finally written to her.

She wrote back: "You know, I am a princess. Where are you, my prince?"

Anjali tied the message to one of the dove's legs. The bird took off gently. As Anjali watched it, she tearfully thought, "This is my angel of God, my divine messenger."

She mindfully travelled back to the time when the Master had explained the essence of messages. Today, his words made sense to her: "Every message has a certain degree of sweetness and a certain import of care. In a message, there is an implicit degree of trust on either side and an openness to receive the other. A message is a silent prayer answered from within the labyrinths of a higher reality, and therefore, a message comes with a lot of responsibility and enriches the receiver in many ways. It is the ultimate gesture of belongingness and love. It also communicates and ties a bond, which exists between the sender and the receiver, and which is revealed with fondness through the message." He had cautioned, "A message, if treated carelessly, can be in vain and the potency in it can be lost instantly. Therefore, there is a great responsibility on the receiver attached to such communication so that the full value of the message and the feeling with which it is sent can be absorbed for one's own sake."

Anjali experienced joy and pain, longing and insecurity, hope and anxiety in her being, all at once. She had waited, longingly, for months after her return from the observatory. Her heart started beating faster and her breath became heavier. She had known that she would hear from the prince but she had not known how. At last, he had sent her a message. She knew he must have asked the Master for her address.

The prince's message put her doubts to rest and doubled her anxiety at the same time. She waited impatiently while she convinced herself that she was heading towards her mission. The sadness from her heart eased somewhat, even as she felt the urgency of wanting to meet the prince. She understood then that it was a strange human failing that makes human beings want more, and always more, and more—an addictive appetite that is never satiated and only increases.

chapter 11

Dream

That night Anjali saw the prince in her dream. He stood against the clouds in the sky, revelling in his regal form.

"Come to my castle," he extended his invitation to her. Then, as if from nowhere, his horse came galloping and stood in front of him. He mounted the horse, lifted her onto it, and the horse galloped away.

The horse unfolded its wings and began to fly. Anjali could see angels in the sky. She thought she could recognize some, she thought she saw her friend, the angel of hope. The angel of hope smiled at her and disappeared in an instant. Anjali knew that Hope had this strange habit of appearing from nowhere, luring one and then disappearing once they felt reassured. Hope enjoys this game.

Anjali had once asked her friend, "Dear Hope, why do you play this game ever so often?" Hope had disappeared without a response.

Seeing Hope in her dream made Anjali believe that it was not actually a dream.

As she dreamt, she saw herself gliding through the stars along with the prince. She was happy; the sky was flooded with shooting stars. At this point, the prince started losing control of his horse. He tried to regain his grip, but the harder he tried, the more he lost control. The horse refused to obey him. The prince was also briskly losing his regal form. Wrinkles appeared on his face that marred his handsomeness. Anjali was frightened. She saw him become translucent like a ghost; then he turned to dust and there was no prince.

Anjali saw herself standing alone. All of a sudden, a noose dropped from above as black shadows appeared around her. They laughed at her and a voice proclaimed, "You are sentenced to death."

She wondered...

From far echoes of time,
Unrelated thoughts chain me,
Forming a noose around my neck,
I wonder, whether it was this that has sentenced me to death?

She tossed and turned in her bed, penetrating her inner vision through the depths of the skies, trying to comprehend the dream. She saw herself moving among souls who had been condemned. She heard confused, helpless voices speak randomly, in pain.

She tried to console the voices, but to no avail. They kept repeating, "We are condemned! We are condemned!"

Anjali asked them, "Who has condemned you?"

The voices replied, "The one who judges us."

That sounded familiar to Anjali. Yes, she herself felt the same way. Who was this who judged? Anjali did not want to leave the voices crying so inconsolably. She tried to speak to them but they gradually grew softer and fainter and soon melted away.

Still in a dream state, she saw herself move into another beautiful space. The outer walls were made of ivory and inside it appeared to be an asylum. There were several persons, all seemingly dead. Some stood motionless, staring endlessly into the skies, while others stood still with their hands flung towards the sky and fingers pointing up. Still others looked at screens placed before them. There was an eerie stillness.

One of them whispered into Anjali's ears, "Please don't disturb us. We have been appointed to balance the earth and the sky. We are balancing it on our little finger and if we move, the entire sky with all its stars will fall. The earth will crumble and with this great fall, mankind will be destroyed. We carry a great responsibility. Do not question us. Do not disturb us."

Anjali asked him, "If all of you are doing your work so perfectly, how is it that the sky rained fire a few minutes ago?"

He replied, "Someone like you must have disturbed us. Please, oh please, I beg of you, don't disturb us."

Anjali stood there and observed them for a long time, wondering whether they were real and whether what they revealed to her was true. She saw another form appear, which started taking the shape of the prince. The prince looked grimly at Anjali. He too seemed to be carrying a great responsibility. He no longer appeared regal and she was frightened to see him. She attempted to speak to him but he said nothing and walked away. Anjali followed him, called out to him. He did not look back.

As she reached out her hand to him, he slapped it away and said, "Do not touch me. I am God. You cannot touch God, go away! Look at me from a distance and build a temple in my name." Anjali could not believe what she heard. She tried again. This time, he roared at her more aggressively. She was visibly shaken.

She wondered again…

In an asylum made of ivory,
Breeds an anxious species,
Afraid of itself?

Anjali looked around at the people in the asylum. They all carried a strange responsibility that she could not comprehend. They thought that they controlled the world. She wondered if they could first control themselves. Anjali wanted to leave the ivory tower but she could not find the way. All the corridors appeared to be the same. Every door led back to the place from where she had started. She forgot how she had entered and wondered whether there was a hidden door that could lead her out of this place. She recalled reading about certain doors that only opened in one direction and that if one entered through them, one could never get out. She was terrified. She thought she had been condemned, maybe forever.

She heard someone say:

Heavens cease to shelter,
And earth no longer comforts.
Furies from the skies,
Rigors of the earth,
Rage into fire and storm.

Anjali looked up and saw two birds fly by. She felt a gentle breeze caress her face as she noticed her friend Hope. Much to her relief, Hope handed her a golden-white petal. She became confident that there was a way out. She experienced joy again as she heard the roar of lions. Anjali found herself out in the open sky. The stars looked even more precious now and she thought:

The lions rage,
Caved in cracks of time,
Sanctuaries of virtue assert!

She understood what she had just experienced.

This life,
To escape into a web of eternity,
Into an endless stream of time.
To revel in the dance of Shiva,
And spin into a chain of hope.

To be lost to one's own self, in order to find meaning of life,
To erode woods that lie on the way,
To hide in a million caves,
To be desperate to find a twig of peace.

To subscribe to norms of the world,
To experience a dazzle of sunshine, a touch of Midas,
To lord over bounties,
And yet one day find that one is less than a speck.

To end, to begin, to end again,
Again, again, and yet again!

Anjali woke up with a start. She felt something soft cupped in her palm. It was the same golden-white petal that Hope had given her. "It was not a dream," she exclaimed as she observed the petal. But as her nose touched the petal, it melted. She saw that it was only a drop of water on which the first rays of the rising sun had cast a spell. "So it was a dream after all, or was it reality?" she pondered.

As she sipped her morning coffee, she mulled over the Master's words of wisdom about dreams. He had explained to his disciples, "A dream is the surfacing of the subconscious. Dreams can be significant in many ways and foretell a future event, or bring into expression a whole gamut of ideas and situations of which the consciousness has no awareness."

He had further elaborated, "A dream moves over a trajectory—a relatively happy path, with some excitement and hope, that may become turbulent. A dream springs out of the seeds of the ego in the conscious part of your mind and plays with the mind, relating historical incidents and memories with intuitive projections of the future."

Just then she heard someone playing the flute. There was magic in the music. She got up from the chair and swayed to the tune.

She went to the window and saw a familiar figure seated on a bench, playing the flute. Her heart skipped a beat as she recognized the person on the bench. It was the prince.

chapter 12

Love

The prince had come to her town on a visit. Even though he met her every day, he made no promises to her. Anjali was happy when she was with him, but every time the prince left her, she was full of pain and doubt. As the days passed, Anjali began to feel alone even in the prince's company. She felt a pain growing in her heart.

The prince never revealed anything about himself. But Anjali was not concerned about not knowing any details about his background. All that mattered to her was that he was the prince.

Yet she began to feel increasingly helpless in his presence. She felt as though the prince was not only in control of himself but also had control over her. She was losing herself to her emotions. She would stay awake all night pining for him and each morning she would hurriedly go to him.

Finally, one day, she lay upon his bed, waiting for his embrace. The prince took her in his arms and repeatedly made love to her. She whispered in her moment of ecstasy...

I wait for thy embrace,
As it fills me with thee,

I wait like an open shell,
Waiting for that one drop, which forms the pearl,
In one precious moment of time

I wait like earth parched in drought
Waiting for the rain, which gifts fertility,
In one precious moment of time

Waiting for years and lifetimes too,
I curl upon myself,
Into galaxies

Into your arms I curl,
Waiting still for thee,
Longing for a sacred union
To preserve thee and me

Like a mystic,
Pledging life for wine,
Intoxicated in me,
Love flows desperately

This time thou art the sakhi,
And I the wait

This time thy filleth my glass,
Again, yet again,
Till the night remains

I pray, my love,
Thou soak me in fullness,
Drunk, I crave
More, and yet more of you

I cease,
I then exist,
I cease yet again,
I then exist once again,
Only to die once again.

In one night I live many aeons,
Many lifetimes.

In a single night I journey many worlds,
Ecstatic, I tirelessly tire myself,
To live life to its brim,
To experience timelessness.

Infinitely in love,
In servile opulence of unlimited desire,
I revel.

I am pleasure,
Thy muse of love and lust,
Unto dust.

I am magic,
Bright and more,
I echo rhymes that encore.

I yearn,
And in pain of yearning,
I am faint in fragrance,
My mind is squandered.

In carnal pleasures that God for humans plans,
Entrapped thus in thee,
Yet again I live in thee.

I dream of thee,
I dream of thy embrace,
I dream yet again,
I dream thou ride again and again on me.

Oh! It must not end,
Not this moment,
Nor many more,
That I seek,
Again, and yet again.

Anjali's head reeled, her heart was fulfilled. She felt that the prince was madly in love with her and wanted her more and more. She looked at the stars as they stood witness to all the moments of wild ecstasies that returned repeatedly through the night. Being with the prince was her sole purpose, and everything else was an illusion. She looked at the prince and saw an overpowering madness in his eyes that pierced through her. She could not lose him now, not for a moment, not ever again. She could not let him go. He must stay, if only so that she could reclaim all the years of yearning.

When the day bled and the prince tired himself out, he turned away and told Anjali, "It is late. You should go home." Anjali was surprised, pained by his abrupt behaviour.

She hurriedly got dressed and headed home with a heavy heart.

When she met the prince the next day, he seemed withdrawn. Anjali wished for the magic to repeat, but he looked at her with a certain awkwardness. She suddenly felt a distance between her and the prince, which seemed to increase with each passing day.

"Is he really the same prince I had seen from the heavens? Is this the same prince for whom I took birth?" Anjali asked herself in exasperation. Life began to stagnate, began to lose meaning. Anjali wondered about the impossibility of the situation. "What is the meaning of all this? Why do I feel forsaken in the company of the prince? Why does my heart ache so much when he is around?"

She was losing control of everything around her. She walked as if in a dream. The waking moments were tinged with a certain unreality, only the pain and the doubt seemed real. She was beginning to understand what the Master had meant when he had said, "I will grant you your wish, but not for the taste of pleasure."

Her relationship with the prince felt hollow. She wondered, "Does the prince just meet me to cope with his loneliness in this town?"

Finally, she mustered the courage to confront him:

Burning streams of moments that chain time,
I burn life into ashes of smoky days.

Burning thus I wonder,
How would you feel if today were the last time you see me?
How would you feel if I were to say,
"I love you, and loving you, destroy myself?"

Will there be a pain that in all its vigour,
Shall claim you for a mission higher?

Or, will it be that day after tomorrow,
You shall know me only as a dream?
As a thing past, and forgotten forever?

The prince had not expected this question. He regarded Anjali for a long time and saw that she waited for an answer anxiously. He saw her against the many colours of the sunset; she was not beautiful, but there was something charming about her. The prince felt a deep attraction for her. Was it love? He knew that he could not lie. He must say something.

And so he spoke:

Measuring life with coffee spoons,
I shall measure myself once again.
Measure-for-measure I shall return the sword that bleeds time.

The prince shrewdly evaded the question. Anjali tried to find hope in what he said but she knew she should not lie to herself. She understood that the prince was not prepared to commit his life to her. Devastated, she wondered, "How could I have gone so wrong? Have I not been born to find his love? Why am I going through this? Why is he so evasive?"

Ever since the prince came to her, she had become self-centred and selfish. She had lost her sensitivity for those who cared for her. The prince's presence had stripped her of her original kindness. She was irritable. She forgot the technique of concentrating on her breath. Each time she tried to practice, her mind wandered, chasing the prince. It rode the horse that would lead her to the castle she had seen from the sky. She was sad and unhappy.

The prince left without saying a word. All along, Anjali had expected this to happen.

One night, while lying on her bed, she tried to observe her breath, which seemed like an impossibility. Suddenly, she felt a dark shadow push her down with its weight. Its form was huge and grotesque. She tried to lift herself up but she could not. She called out to the prince for help and the shadow became heavier. She felt herself being strangled and tried to cry out for help, but her voice failed her. Then she remembered the Master and implored him for his help. The weight lifted, she felt a soft breeze touch her face and the horror was gone.

She knew that someone or something unnatural had visited her. As she calmed herself, she reflected, "The thought of the prince aggravated the weight. My real saviour is the Master, and the divine linkage through him."

She looked at herself in the mirror and spoke carefully, examining each word:

Love line bent now and again,
A churning and a whirlpool,
My boat is caught,
Now only he can spew this wreck.

When in search I waited for love,
Waiting was intense,
And separation longed for a reason.

Now tied, I wait for my destiny,
To show a way which will stop this wait.

Caught in a mesh, I long to be out of it,
Alone, or with him, but out of it.
Maybe love has its own blues,
In it, or out of it, it does not exist.

She heard echoes of the word "exist." She looked out at the stars journeying across the sky.

Her heart longed for a lost dream. Life had teased her. At that moment, she recollected what the corpse in the tribal village had revealed to her, "The prince does not exist."

Her subconscious stirred, reminding her of someone... Someone who had told her a long time ago, "You seek a love that is only for you. You seek a mirage in which water is only an illusion. You are like the fragrant kasturi deer who chases the fragrance to the end of the jungle and tired, falls asleep."

Anjali wondered, "Despite all of the warnings, why did I wait and long for the prince? The prince left as suddenly as he arrived and took with him my happiness and peace. Till I met him, I lived in hope. Now I am left feeling cheated and belittled. The pain of an unrequited love wounds me deeply."

As tears rolled down her cheeks, she kept repeating, "It does not exist. It does not exist." The winds echoed, "Exist... exist... exist..." Time went by and the gentle echoes of the wind helped her fall asleep.

That night, in her dreams, she saw the prince getting married. The bride wore white, mourning with a baby in her arms. Anjali also dreamt of a lost land—a lost Shangri-La of hope. As the dream collapsed, there was ash everywhere.

She woke up, reflecting about her dream.

A dream that was just taking shape,
Of a Shangri-La emerging from a lost horizon,
'Ere, a dream melts again,
Gliding with a breath, which lost its track,
In a gallop that vanished in the dark,
To thence, where there was nothing but ashes.

She slid back in deep slumber and saw herself walking through a dark valley immersed in deathly silence and scattered ash. She searched for the prince but to no avail.

Her head felt extremely heavy when she woke up. But, she hurriedly got dressed and went to the *kund*. While gazing at the water, she wondered:

What offer does the future have?
What pain yet to be lived?
Which friendship yet to be feigned?
Which love yet to be trusted?

As Anjali looked on, she became aware of someone gazing back at her. The gaze beckoned her, and then there was a ripple in the water. The water wrinkled, and, with it, the gaze. The water stilled again; the gaze stilled and looked back at Anjali again. This prompted Anjali to write the following lines on the shore:

I gaze at a gaze,
Which, gazing at me,
Beckons and reveals choicelessness.

She told herself, "I cannot be choiceless. I made my choice and I am suffering because of it. There is always suffering associated with a choice. People make choices, and I too made a choice."

Anjali no longer wanted to stay at home, as the comfort from her family seemed like a burden. She decided to go to a faraway place so that she could be free to feel miserable. So she applied for a post at the academy. "Intellectual stimulation at the academy could reward me with peace," she thought.

She waited restlessly for a response from the academy.

The letter of appointment finally arrived, much to her relief. Her family was happy for her and proud of the posting, even though they were saddened to see her go.

Anjali was looking forward to it and yet a part of her already missed all that she was leaving behind—her family, the discussions with her sister and the times spent contemplating at the *kund*.

The evening before she was to leave, Anjali stood at her bedroom window, looking at the setting sun. She wondered, "When will I return to stand here and admire the sunset? What kinds of changes will I return to? Will the prince visit me at the academy? I know he will not. I know I have to mortgage my life to an illusion. Destiny has decided my journey."

She felt a breeze from the sea and it soothed her nerves. She heard the waves rising and ebbing and assured herself, "I shall return to the rising and ebbing waves."

A song by Paul Anka echoed from a distant spring in her heart as she sang:

Liners across the sea,
Sailors on shore,
Fighters soaring in air,
Cups in coffee shops,
Love is a lonely song.

Banquets full of guests,
Mountains bereft of quests,
Ages turning dark,
Stars wearing out like candles in the sky,
Yet seconds of beckoning, sing a song,
Love is a lonely song.

Day and night, night and day,
Cleaning my heart with a song,
Send a letter within a corn,
He will never be the way I thought,
Love is a lonely song.

Friends go like autumn leaves,
Friends drop like teardrops from an eye,
Friends fall as evening by a night,

Friends go,
Love is a lonely song.

Gold drops from lit lamps in streets,
As raindrops fall from a sky,
Gold scatters on metal roads,
As sodium lights wash metal gates,
Gold is in my heart,
As love sings a lonely song.

Look at a falling star,
Listen to its music till it falls,
Listen, and let it pierce your heart,
Listen, love is within,
Love is not a lonely song.
Love is not a song.

Tears rolled down her cheeks, the pain in her heart hurt her soul. But she did not have time to mourn her unrequited love. She had a farewell party to attend.

Even though she made an effort to enjoy the party Sara had organized, she could not help but notice, through the night, how the varied tunes of music played affected her inner world. The melodious tunes built a tempo that climaxed and then abruptly collapsed when the tracks changed.

After the party, she returned to her room and contemplated, "We are all slaves of the external world. We are slaves to our senses." She wrote in her journal:

Music overwhelms the vivacity of life,
The party continues,
Building into a climax,
Then all at once,
Dropping to the depths of an existential abyss.

A tune flows into octaves of delight,
And then a form contoured,
Breaks into a continuity of thoughts.

Would reconciliation overtake norms of human existence?
Which shattered, or questioned,
Would recreate a significance deeper in the soul?

The glass mountain must be shattered,
If only to build a glass house, which casts an illusion,
Of a delicate warmth whence a furnace glows.

Only people inside are glass dolls,
Ornamental in value.
But fragile,
The showpieces break,
As the real comes to life.

The pain was unbearable, the memory of the glass mountain unwelcome. She yearned for the prince's love, or her liberation from it.

She tried to reach out to the prince—in her mind, in her thoughts, in her heart. Looking at him from her mind's eye, she said:

We stretched our hands in the dark, my friend,
And a fog melted away,
Light of a day shone,
Warmth lit our hearts,
Joy echoed from a past,
Were we then strangers, my friend?

Silent looks,
I looked again,
A longing seemed to shift,
Time came back from a time long past.

How strange,
This mortal heart,
That being moved,
Was like a storm.

Tossed, like a wave against you,
Tossed, against a rock,
I cried and screamed,
Yet music flowed.

We passed into unknown,
The familiarity of friendship,
And crushed a rose in our hands.

We looked once again,
And dismissed a thundering doubt.

Estranged,
We parted as strangers, my friend,
And once again we let lightning pass.

Hope

Anjali was not at peace. She saw her friend, the angel of hope, come again and then she saw her go. Seeing Hope walk away, Anjali felt her heart sink within her. She called out to Hope, she searched for a falling star to make a wish for Hope. She scanned the sky for a long time but there was no falling star; suddenly, she saw Hope flying speedily across the sky.

Anjali asked her:

Amid pain and despair, is there Hope?
Recalcitrant in its vigour, does she snap?

Hope replied:

The Tao of void clamours for space,
And abruptly the centre gapes,
Yawning, hope takes to wing,
And …

Anjali completed the sentence:

She escapes.

Hope pointed to the sky and said:

"These stairs lead to the stars,
As moon brackets the sun,
Inmates rush to the doors,
Aspirations take roots,
But channelled through status quo, life moves."

Hope disappeared, leaving Anjali alone with her thoughts.

As I look around, in search of Hope,
I stumble in a cemetery,
As I grope my way through the dead,
I see graves fortify a resort,
And from the resort, I see Hope deftly try an escape.

Lonely hearts form a ring around choked pubs,
And as they lift a glass to toast,
They repeat,
"There would be time still to revise,"
Dear old Satan rises,
Cheering all,
Wishes human race a disgrace,
Clamouring thus for a wild embrace,
It wishes God and goodness a final blow,
Hope stalls,
As she steps through corpse, bones, and all, she escapes.

Alma mater outlines a resort,
Was she right to leave her corridors?
And from equations, and stars,
Step down to descend on earth?
Was it right that I moved pawns,

When on the chessboard the king was at stake?
And again right at that moment, when stalemated
I revelled in glory, as if a game was won?
I lost the game,
And alas, I saw Hope escape.

I wait for letters to come,
And put a spell on this day,
I wait for desires to blossom,
I wait to discover that silent darkness in a rose,
That makes life so full of grace,
And as I wait, I wonder if I wait for Hope to escape.

My acts are once again put on an anvil,
And with hammering of every blow,
Pain journeys to the heart,
Obsessed, I step down from this stage,
A tired protagonist,
I see smoke rings circle all around,
I see ash in my palms,
The future burning in latent storms.
As I wait to welcome trouble,
Secretly hoping to see Hope again,
I wonder if Hope has yet escaped.

The sky is still the limit,
And I wait for it to fall,
Hoping that then entrapped,
Between heaven and earth,
Hope would return to earth,
Or if crushed,
I wonder would she still remain the same?
In silent cynicism,

I see Hope leave grooves in my mind,
I see her wander like a vagabond,
I see her in a stray desire,
Till I cry, "Hope,"
Has she escaped?

I fall to my knees,
On wounded pride,
And looking for craters in Wonderland,
I wonder if I could journey to the stars,
Or see hope dwelling in voids within,
I wonder, but I find no castles in the air,
Nor, my prince coming down the stairs,
In schizophrenic existence,
As I paint vultures, and life,
In reckless fever,
I think, once again disguised,
Hope has escaped.

Anjali felt despair and an unfathomable loneliness. These words flowed through her:

A noose around my neck tightens its grip,
Life seems to pass out.
As I stretch my arms to it,
And offer gold,
Spurning gold, life asks,
"Would you pay my price?"

I ask for its price,
And life answers,
"Lo! My price is, thou shalt not question life."

I give my word to pay the price.
The noose around my neck loosens its grip,
And as an enticing alternative, death seems to dip,
As if condemning me to eternal life,
Life condemns me not to question life.

I wonder am I condemned to a life of Sisyphus?
Questioning Hope, I stretch my arms to call death back,
But vanished in a mist,
With it, I see Hope escape.

Teased by life,
Now that it bought me at a price,
It plays with me like a beetle with a bee,
Abandoning me all at once,
It beckons, "Lo! Find for yourself an excuse, to live again.
In despair, find where Hope has gone again,
Search, for Hope has lost its way."

As I grope in doubt, and darkness,
I find a fortress, and a prison door,
I hear anguished cries,
I hear clanking of chains,
Amid this, a whisper says,
It is Hope that has escaped.

And I am reminded at this moment, the words of the Buddha,
"Life is a suffering,
And, desire the root cause of suffering."
"Be a light unto thyself."

Helpless, she searched for something to cling to for support. She then remembered the talisman her grandfather had given her as a farewell gift when she was leaving for the observatory. He had told her, "If you are ever lost, even to yourself, this talisman will protect you." Anjali opened her cupboard to search for it. She had never used it before because she had been far too confident to ever need it. Yet, today, she looked for it frantically. She searched for it everywhere, over and over again. Angrily, she told herself, "It is gone." She gave up on the search as her mind returned to her grandfather's words when he had handed over the talisman to her: "If you don't take care of it, it will be gone. There are powers looking out for the talisman and they can wish it away, if they deem it necessary."

Tearfully, she prayed to the talisman's invisible protectors, "Please forgive me for being so careless with the talisman. Please return it to me now as I need it desperately." As she wiped her tears, she felt an invisible force guide her to a purse stowed away in the cupboard. She opened it and found the talisman safely tucked away in a small inner pocket.

Anjali took it in her hands and prayed. Her mind was abuzz. Still holding the talisman to her bosom, she walked to the window and looked at the sky. Something flashed across the sky, what seemed like a falling star. With a lump in her throat, she wished for peace and prayed again. As tears continued rolling down her face, she felt a painful throb in her head. It built up and soon became so unbearable that she felt like she would lose consciousness any moment. She wished it would happen soon.

Something moved across the sky again. It seemed like Hope. Her face brightened and she wondered…

Do miracles happen all at once?
Does Hope appear once again?
I look at the neglected talisman,

And through passages of time,
I hear church bells ring loud,
I know, Hope hides somewhere within.

Must I stop or build a home with ascendance on its wings?
And ambling on a hopeless course, recapture Hope within?

Must I stop,
Or like an eagle perch high on mountain tops?
And wild and fierce,
Madly find a board,
Where Hope has escaped?

Must I let it go, or convene a meeting with hell, earth and sky?
In now and here,
To capture Hope,
To tie her wings,
To chain her to my soul,
And then to know,
Hope, alas, in all its freedom lies in faith within.

The talisman had worked its miracle. Hope had found her way into Anjali's heart. Even though Anjali knew she would never see the prince again, her pain began to ease.

Her being was scarred, but not her soul—of that she was certain. "With faith comes an undying hope. A hope that love will silently wait for me inside the sanctum sanctorum of my heart, dormant and patient."

chapter 14

Search

The journey to the academy was long, through forests and spiralling roads, waterfalls and distant clouds that rolled over the mountain tops. Anjali travelled through the beauties of nature, through the sombre afternoon and the setting sun, through the mist and the clouds, through pain and endurance, through courage and defeat. She was on a journey full of the varied colours and emotions of life. She journeyed through an existence that carried the odour of burning sweat and the scent of heavenly breeze. But above all, it carried a message: "All must change."

The hills were lined with purple and yellow foxgloves and wild grass swaying in the breeze. How rooted they were; how flexible and willing to change; how humble in their bending movements, these true creations of God.

Anjali tried speaking to them as the bus moved on the spiralling roads. She asked them their names, their age and if they had ever suffered in love.

The foxgloves replied, "We know no suffering in love. Love cannot make us suffer."

Surprised, Anjali asked, "Have you ever loved at all?"

The foxgloves responded, "We have done nothing in our lifetimes but love, love and love."

Anjali implored, "Did you find your love reciprocated?"

The foxgloves did not understand the question. "What is reciprocation in love?"

Anjali explained, "When you love someone and that someone loves you back."

The foxgloves asserted, "We never thought that could be the purpose of love. When we love, we only love. Why should we want someone else to love in return?"

Anjali was surprised, "How else do you find fulfilment and satisfaction in love?"

The foxgloves: "Our love gives us the fulfilment and the satisfaction. Love is its own fulfilment and its own satisfaction."

Amused, Anjali teased them, "Do you love other foxgloves or do you love the breeze? Do you love the wild bees or do you love the cold frost? Whom do you love?"

The foxgloves replied, "We never differentiate. We love everyone and everything that we come in contact with, and we love all of them equally and well. Human beings are strange creatures, indeed and ask strange questions. We have no boundaries, we know no boundaries. We know we are all God's creation so we love all. We love the mud and the algae, we love the ants and the insects, we love the breeze and the sunshine, we love the wind and the frost, we love those who caress us and also those who crumple us. We do not differentiate in our love."

"How can you love those who crumple you?" Anjali was astonished.

The foxgloves explained, "We have to love them because they have been sent to us for a purpose. We only know how to surrender to God's will, and we know that every little thing in this universe has a meaning, a purpose. It is predestined. It simply cannot be any other way."

Anjali laughed at them, "You are fatalists, poor things. But I do not blame you. You cannot be anything else. Anyway, I am a human being and I know that I can shape my own destiny."

The foxgloves: "Then why could you not stop the prince?"

Anjali now looked at them with a certain degree of respect. How did they know about the prince? *What* did they know about her and the prince?

With a smile, the foxgloves said, "We have no ego and, therefore, we stretch ourselves into all beings. We flow with the breeze, we shine with the sunshine, we melt with the dewdrops, we freeze with the frost. We breathe with your breath, we smile with your hopes, we perish with your tears. We are one with all, we know you."

They urged her, "Go to the academy. You will find many answers and you will learn how little you can wield your destiny."

The bus came to a halt and woke Anjali up. It was her drop-off point. From there she walked a short distance to the academy gates. The academy was scattered across a large area that looked almost forsaken. It was thinly forested and barracks were built on different levels of the hillock. The trees were not green, yet they looked strangely artistic. To Anjali, they resembled jilted lovers and she empathized with them. "At least I can share my misery with them," she mused as she walked past them.

The academy's intellectual atmosphere vitalized her spirit and eased her aching heart. But every evening, when Anjali sat by the window in her cottage, the setting sun reminded her of her heartache. She continued to pine for the prince.

One evening, as she sat acknowledging the fires of longing, she recalled the Master's words regarding karma, "Life is all about one's karmas. Karmas of this birth, karmas of past births, karmas born out of action, karmas born out of intentions, even karmas born out of thoughts."

Anjali felt that only by knowing what karmas she suffered from would she be able to find some relief, maybe bear the pain or endure this suffering. "But what is it? How could I ever find out? I need to search."

The word "search" rang a bell as she recalled the Master's discourse, "Search is a quest into the meaning of it all. One does not search what they know. In a search, one is required to be open to the unexpected and the unknown. The search begins with a surrender to that intuitive power, which will reveal itself on its own only if one allows it to surface. Search is, therefore, one of the simplest ways to progress. At the same time, it is fraught with complications that arise from one's own ego. Search requires harmony between the mind, heart and spirit to progress towards one's destination."

The Master's golden words made her resolve to meditate every day, so that her ego would melt away, allowing her to welcome the unknown and lead her into the depths where her destination was stationed.

However, meditation brought her no relief. In fact, it seemed to aggravate her misery. She became increasingly impatient. One evening, as she sat on her mat to meditate, she exclaimed, "This cannot go on, it must stop!"

The lines from Yeats' poem kept revolving in Anjali's mind as she found herself in an incomparable mess. As she settled into her breath, she implored:

Why this silence and the longing?
Why does distance in emptiness gape?

Why do echoes build a bridge,
Into an illusion that I mistake as real?

Why in a buried past, music melts a grave?

Alas, in casual abandon,
*Things fall apart, and the centre cannot hold.**

I wonder,
What is it that so fills my days with mystic uneasiness?
I cease all at once, negating existence,
I lose my roots,
Things fall apart, and the centre cannot hold.

All at once, the street lights, the rumbling of the cars,
All melt into a tune of fervour,
And, in fever I shout,
"Is it all real?"
Back comes the echo,
Real, real, real!
But I know it is fever,
And, things fall apart, the centre cannot hold.

Like a satellite I revolve,
Do I rotate?
Do I have a light of my own?
Why then I walk in loneliness,
Trying to grope for friends?
Love parts its way, and declares,
Things fall apart, the centre cannot hold.

In mute surrender, I see my escape,
But stuck in grooves, tiers do not move,

* Inspired by the lines from William Butler Yeats' poem *The Second Coming*.

Like a creeper I twine along the roofs,
In solemn steps,
I hear time march,
Once again, I discern the breaking of line,
Alas, things fall apart, the centre cannot hold.

I hold my breath and watch the movement of stars,
Like an outlaw I journey underground,
And as fever melts this heart,
I hear despair declare,
Things fall apart, the centre cannot hold.

Struck by arrows of love,
The march has a softer rhyme.
Feeling ill at ease I realize,
Things have fallen apart, and alas, the centre was never there to hold.

Like a void I escape the miracle of time,
But, wounds remain unhealed.
As I journey in blood,
Murky storms propel me to swim towards the whirlpool,
And, in its vacuous centre I realize,
Why things fall apart, and the centre cannot hold.

Has comprehension become so absurd?
Has the eternal river lost its way?
And losing it, does it march to the eye of a storm?
Does it then declare:
"Things fall apart, and the centre cannot hold."

At that moment, she knew she must realize her true self, which would liberate her. She heard a voice gently remind her, "The true self is pure. The true self is joyful. The true self knows no misery because the true self is a part of God. The true self is not insecure."

"But where should I start my search?" Anjali wondered as she stared blankly at the setting sun. Once again, the Master's words came flowing to her, "You are a blessed soul. You will always find the answers whenever you seek them. Always remember, the search should be earnest. You must go to the roots of your suffering. You must learn about the roots of your longing."

The Master's explanations always helped her find solace and at that moment, they assured her that she could actually begin her search. "The search," the Master had explained one day, "is an experiment of the soul and a journey that, in many ways, helps one find the central meaning, which will create harmony and resonance within."

...

The next day Anjali woke up before dawn, waiting for the sun's rays to break free from the teeth of the night. Slowly, steadily, gently, a soothing pink and golden hue coloured the sky. The first rays of sunshine filtered through her being, and the early morning mist refreshed and stilled her soul. She spread out a mat and sat on it with her legs crossed. She shut her eyes and observed her breath.

Her breath revealed to her the words of the Bible, "Truth will set you free." Anjali reflected on this wisdom. She remembered her divine origin, albeit briefly, as it hurriedly slipped from her memory.

In the wilderness of her inner world, she realized that there is always a way. She felt a chill through her spine as she mulled about this path, and she knew she would tread upon it.

chapter 15

Regression

Anjali sat before the crystal reader. Her heart was beating fast. The crystal reader entered into a trance as the air slowly grew heavy with the unnatural scent of herbs burning in the room. A strange green mist surrounded the crystal, then it lit up with a blue tinge and then, the crystal turned white as snow.

The crystal reader revealed:

Forked emotions like a serpent's tongue,
Vicious in their intent, poison life, fatally.

Vitality and exuberance,
A zest for life seems to evade,
Turmoil lies within.

Meaning of life, almost moth-bitten,
Vacuous and corroded, hides behind appearances,
Feigning to overpower the innate.

Desolate fatalism,
Almost teleological,
Basks reality in insanity.

Clouded by a misguided intelligence,
Appearances convey something more than what is.

An imagination hallucinates into a wilderness,
Oblivious and insignificant,
As appearances attack life well.

Anjali's fear made her numb as she heard the crystal ball reader. She could see the strange colours from the crystal reflected on the reader's face. The mystical woman looked like a ghost in the pink-purple light of the room.

The crystal reader continued, "I see a wild forest. I see a desert. I see a forest beyond the sands of a desert. It is wild. It is fearful. It is beautiful. I see a star glitter. I see a falling star. I see a girl child born. I see a tribe. I see the tribe crowning the baby girl with a bejewelled crown. I see the tribal men and women come and kneel in front of her. I see the girl in her early teens now, seated on a stone chair at a great height and I see all the men and women dancing and kneeling in turns before her. There is a big fire and there is hot food. The tribals dance wildly and there is an unnatural celebration. I see the people crown the girl child; I see them mark her with their blood. Suddenly, I hear loud salutations, 'Oh *Amba*! Oh *Amba*!' The girl child is ordained the goddess of the tribe. I see the crowned goddess wave her hand to them and they all stop. In unison, they all kneel before her in awe. I see them sit and distil wine and liquor in their hearths. I see the tribals happy. I see the girl child grow up. She is a woman now. She is the goddess of the tribe."

The crystal ball gazer paused for a moment and then continued, "Yet I see the goddess looking sad and perpetually in search. She is beautiful. I see her smile. I see her body glow like gold. I feel the warmth of her love. I hear the footsteps of a horse. I see a handsome man dressed like a prince on the horse. I can see his black heart. The man shoots an arrow at a wild deer. The deer groans and dies. I see all the tribals surround him. They want to know who shot the arrow in their forest. I see the tribals surround the man. They all have poisoned arrows drawn on him. They are breathing heavily."

After a brief pause she went on, "Now I see the goddess approach in all her grandeur. She climbs the steps to her stone chair. She stands there. I see the tribals await her judgment. The prince looks harassed. The goddess sits unmoved on the stone chair and stares at the prince. I see the prince kneel before her. I see anxiety in his eyes. He entreats the goddess and I see the heart of the goddess melt. I see the goddess descend from her pedestal. As she comes down, she keeps her gaze fixed on the prince. She takes his hand and lifts him up. I see a sudden lightning. There is thunder and storm."

She stopped to look at Anjali and then shifted her eyes back to her crystal ball. "I hear the galloping of horses. I see the prince on his horse. The goddess is in his arms. She has yielded to his dark charms. It is a cold winter night. I can hear the sounds of a storm. I cannot see anything. It is all gone."

Anjali heaved a long sigh. The mist that had surrounded the crystal ball started to thin out and was soon gone. The room was clear again. The reader's face returned to normal—she was out of her trance.

All that the reader had revealed held an undeniable grip on Anjali. She grew restless.

...

That night Anjali dreamt that she was in a forest. She saw the prince standing in front of her. Then she saw him galloping away on a majestic horse with her. The horse unfolded its wings and began to fly. It was a familiar dream, but this time she saw herself entering a castle in the dark of the night. The air was sinister and she was thrown into a room, which was then locked from the outside. Anjali woke up in a fright. She knew that this was the aftermath of her visit to the crystal reader and she reprimanded herself for going there.

Anjali assured herself, "Whatever the crystal reader said was a figment of her imagination. After all, she had to say something intriguing, maybe even something that did not make sense, just something that would compel me to go back to her. But I will not go back. I have no links to any tribe, nor am I a goddess. My visit to the crystal reader has shaken my entire being. This is unnatural."

The next day, Anjali found it difficult to focus at the academy. The incomplete story intrigued her. The sight of the galloping horse and the prince carrying the goddess haunted her. She cajoled herself yet again, "It is a fictitious piece of the crystal ball gazer's imagination, and it has no connection to me. I should not have been so weak-minded in the first place. I was foolish to go to the fortune teller, to carry out my search in a regression visualized by this woman."

However, every night she continued to dream of the prince carrying her away on his horse. Finally, desperate, she decided to go back to the crystal ball gazer to discover the rest of her story.

The reader refused to entertain Anjali. Bluntly, she told her, "I will not go any further with you." Anjali persisted and the reader gave in with a warning, "If you wish to know more, be absolutely certain that you are endangering yourself. You are forcing me to share a secret that must not be known."

Even though Anjali felt this was a gimmick, she agreed. She needed to know everything the mystical woman could find in her crystal ball. She assured the fortune teller, "I am prepared to come face to face with every secret of my past. Only truth can set me free."

The reader made one last attempt to caution her, "Whatever the crystal ball will reveal this time will shatter you. You could lose your equilibrium. Scrying is a dark science. While it illuminates the future, it takes you to the depths of the dark past. My crystal ball is my tool of regression, a telescope that shows me a distance beyond comprehension. The bravest, at times, do not recover from the shock of their past. Nature blesses us with amnesia about our past births. We should live with this blessing, rather than open the dark can of worms."

Anjali contested her by revealing what she had heard the Master say regarding scrying and regression, "Regression, through the science of crystal reading, is to hold a crystal and see the many facets reflecting the varied colours of light and knowing all the same that within the crystal, it is the same transparent, colourless material." She further stated, "I felt compelled to see you the first time because I am seeking answers in the past that can help me understand my present. What has linked you and me together is the crystal, the crystal that will give me clarity. The crystal is your tool of regression, it has the power to lead one to a transformation, which causes a qualitative and incredible difference, a break from where one starts. And yet there is continuity because behind the structural change, the elements remain the same."

The crystal ball gazer was convinced that Anjali was ready to know more as she was a student who understood the essence of the Master's words.

The reader burnt the herbs and dimmed the lights in the room. She cast her gaze on her crystal ball and began to slide into a trance. This time the air in the room felt heavier, a heaviness that penetrated Anjali's soul. A mystical orange mist surrounded the crystal. It darkened and turned black.

The crystal ball reader began to speak:

Scepticism injects doubt with apprehension and hurt,
Caves of isolation in morbidity desire ventilation.

Heavens cease to shelter,
And earth no longer comforts,
A fury of sky,
Vigour of earth,
Rage into fire and storm.

In an asylum made of ivory,
Breeds an anxious species,
Afraid of itself.

The lions rage,
Caved in cracks of time,
Sanctuaries of virtue assert.

Though dark, Anjali saw hope at the end. It consoled her.

The reader revealed, "I see a castle hidden in the dark. I see a window. I see someone crying. I am trying to look inside. I cannot see anyone. I hear whispering. I hear a sinister laughter. Then silence."

The crystal ball gazer paused. Her face began to distort, and she waved her hand and shouted, "Stop! Stop! A cold-blooded murder! You will have to bear the cross for many, many lifetimes. Stop! Stop! You shall bear the burden of this act."

Then, as if in agony, she revealed, "He cannot be spared now. The prince has killed the goddess and he rejoices with other women."

The reader continued, "I see the royal priest. The prince pretends to mourn the death of the goddess. I see the royal priest walking away in anger. I see him curse the prince. The goddess is dead! The goddess is dead! I hear the rumblings of a wild storm, as though the earth will be ripped to shreds."

Anjali could no longer hear the reader's voice but she herself could see it all clearly. This was her past life. She was a goddess who had dropped from the skies. She was reliving her past now, in another time span. "The prince had lured me. I was an angel in heaven who yearned for the prince. The prince killed me! Yet again I have relived the pain of betrayal, denial and unrequited love. I have relived death at the hands of the one I love."

This revelation sent a shooting pain through Anjali's heart. Her head throbbed as if it would explode into a thousand pieces. She vomited blood and was soon unconscious.

An ambulance was called.

chapter 16

Faith

Anjali was in a coma in the hospital. Her world had almost ceased in the last 24 hours. She was struggling between life and death. It was a wild night, with the winds whistling ruthlessly through the leaves that cloaked the trees outside the window. It seemed like the storm would shred nature to pieces. It seemed like the messengers of death were desperately knocking on the door. The knocking grew louder as the thunderous roar increased in volume. Anjali was oblivious to all that was happening.

Just then, there was a gentle rap on the door. The door opened and the Master stood there, surrounded by a golden light. With love radiating from his being, he walked towards Anjali and gently touched her forehead. The storm outside abated with a slight thud and the winds began retreating.

Anjali's breath became sturdy and steady, her body stirred. In the struggle between life and death, life won. She wondered where she was and what was happening around her. The Master smiled as he informed her, "Realize you are the world. The world *is* because you are here. You leave the world and the world ceases. Nothing is permanent and nothing is of consequence." He then told her to rest and left the room.

Anjali mulled over these words repeatedly till she grasped their essence. She closed her eyes and observed her breath.

She let the thoughts pass. Her mind steadied, and in a flash she heard the Master say, "You lack faith. A person filled with faith is strong as there is no scope for weakness. A person full of faith is integrated as a whole, there is no scope to be torn and fragmented."

Anjali reflected on these words. She had often prayed to God, she had observed innumerable days of fasting, she had practiced other ways of penance, she had visited temples and monasteries. Would she have done this if she had lacked faith? She questioned herself repeatedly till it dawned on her that, "The Master is right. The praying, the fasting, the penance, the visits to so many temples have all been driven by a purpose. They were all in the hope that I would reach my prince. No, this is not faith!"

"Instead of placing faith in the Creator, I only yearned and prayed for my prince, for a love that would exclusively be mine. I had placed all my trust in the prince. He was my dream, my obsession, my mission; the prince who had murdered me and rejoiced with other women." She gasped as she realized this. Again, she lost consciousness. The nurses frantically attended to her and tried to revive her.

There was a gentle, calming breeze and all at once, the tension in the room eased. Anjali slowly opened her eyes. She heard the calming sound of 'Aum' and looked around the room for the source. She encountered brightness all around and felt a supernatural presence that relaxed her. She felt the warmth of her mother's love and sensed her mother's loving gaze. Anjali fell asleep, safe in her mother's presence.

As she slept, her mind threw vivid images at her. She saw the window of the castle from the sky. She saw the prince at the window. She saw a star fall. She felt herself falling from the bed. She became afraid. Her breath hastened. Her heart ached intensely. As she remembered the Master, she felt his presence. The pain began to ease.

With her mother's loving gaze, the Master's presence and the miracle of the gentle, calming breeze, Anjali began to understand faith. She started observing the pain and other sensations in her body, allowing her breath to help her mind find equanimity. She returned to the spot of pain, which felt less intense. However, her mind eventually returned to the prince, her obsession and betrayal. She observed her breath, which was fast and hot. As she continued to observe it, she witnessed it becoming steady and calm.

Involuntarily and compulsively, her mind kept wandering towards the prince. It remained there for undefined moments till she was aware of it. Again and again, she brought her mind back to her breath and to the sensations in her body. Each time she repeated to herself, "This is all transitory. I shall move towards equanimity."

As she gently shut her eyes, she heard the self ask the soul:

Faith, I seek,
For I am weak.

She heard Soul in the Master's voice reply:

Let me tell you about faith;

Faith is the grace of the universe,
A silent call of divinity,
A wisdom inherited from incarnations,
A prayer from the depths of a being.

The knowledge of God's underlying presence,
A feeling of a touch,
The cuddling in his lap,
A nuzzle into his charisma.

Faith is a belief that asserts,
And a trust that beckons,
And yet more sure than both.

Faith through ashes shines in embers that glow,
Gently unveiling life,
An unexpected show.

Faith is embracing fear,
For it is music sheer,
Singing freedom for the soul,
Faith is words drowned in prayers.

Faith is going deeper, deeper,
And yet deeper within.
Faith is curling into Tao,
Journeying beyond!

Faith is care,
A silent caress,
A revelation that someone cares.

Faith is a silent acceptance,
A transcript from higher vibrations,
A message from the universe,
Subtle, vibrant, divine,
A love that pines,
A beauty that shines.

Faith is the awakening to that essence,
Of he, thou,
And thou, he,
The favoured one!

The Master continued:

Faith is knowing,
Thou art the fragrance,
The essence,
The Creation,
A silent exclamation!

Thou art beauty,
The magnificence,
The spark,
The effulgence!

Thou art the courage of warriors,
The undying love of eternal lovers,
The soul,
The Eternal Self itself!

Thou art the guru,
The dispeller of ignorance.
The valiant knight in his armour,
The chivalry, the bravery!

Thou art the saviour,
And also the saved.
The glory,
And also the glorious!

Thou art time,
And also the timelessness,
Beyond the past and the future,
And also the present!

Thou art love,
The Master.
In everyone,
And also nothing.

Faith is faith,
And no more and no less.
Faith is faith itself.
Faith that all is well
In spite of all not so well.

Faith is life in face of death
Faith is wealth in face of stealth
Faith is success in serial failures
Faith is Self beyond self.

Faith is goodness in a reign of evil,
A trust on the anvil.

Faith is rivers corroding rocks,
Faith is the key to every lock.

Faith is fire,
Faith is ether,
Faith is water,
Faith is zephyr,
Faith is earth,
And all that existed before birth.

Faith has neither mirrors,
Nor has sails,
Yet, it moves mountains, releasing tales.

Faith affirms beauty,
Dispels doubt.
With it, within,
Nature shouts!

Through troubled waters,
Faith wades, as softly as with sunshine,
A dewdrop fades.

Calmly, faith sings in caves,
In gentle voices,
A word that stays.

Still as silence,
Faith washes pain with tears,
Moulding destinies, it fights the spears
Fanning hope, it steers.

Faith speaks the language of love,
Flies every dove.
Lines every cloud with silver and gold
Guards every treasure and all that's bold.

Faith is purity,
Faith is love.
Faith is God alone,
Faith is all sins atoned.

Faith is knowledge,
Faith is wisdom.
Faith is revelation of the unknown,
Faith is a tree standing tall and lone.

Faith, without revealing direction,
Steers you on.
Faith is that state of being,
In which wisdom dawns!

A couple of days later, Anjali asked the nurse about the Master's visit. The nurse informed her, "Nobody except the doctors and hospital staff entered your room. Your mother is the only one who has constantly been by your side." Yet Anjali could feel the Master's presence all the time. She was convinced that she had been restored to life by the Master's touch, and that of the Creator, even as she had lain recovering in her mother's warmth, care and love.

One morning, Anjali woke up to the exuberance of the sunshine. She observed her breath. She cupped her palms and prayed in gratitude. She felt warmth pour into her cupped palms. Then she looked at her mother and thought to herself, "How ridiculous I have been, obsessed with a love that was never there, while I ignored the one that never ceased. The one unconditional love."

In that moment, the Creator, the Master and her mother merged in her vision, losing distinction. Anjali was firm with herself, "They are one, and have always been the One."

Her mother's face lit up as she saw Anjali sit up and smile.

Anjali was soon discharged from the hospital, after a month of recovery and swinging between unconsciousness and consciousness.

She went back to the academy but her mother decided to stay with her for a few months. Anjali felt like a child, pampered and protected. With every passing day, she felt increasingly reassured about life. She felt light and cheerful. With the truth revealed to her, her longing for the prince no longer weighed down her soul. She could appreciate the bounties the Creator had bestowed so liberally upon her. She practiced gratitude heartfully. And the more she expressed her gratitude, the more blessed she felt. With every moment of gratitude, her heart became lighter and her mind more focused.

Anjali immersed herself in her research and worked with an unparalleled energy. Her soul had been set free and her concentration for her work was now complete. She was filled with the faith about which the Master had once instructed her.

The Master had revealed, "When there is faith, the self gets an opportunity to express itself in all its glory, and helps the smaller self integrate with the Self through self-awareness. With faith, a different dimension of reality comes into reckoning, which is safe, secure and vibrant. It is a reality in which you can be yourself and unfold all your potentials without being judged."

He had elaborated, "Faith is the innocent leap of a child into the arms of her mother, without fearing even for a moment that she would lose her life. Faith is the strong conviction that you are guided, protected, loved, cared for and accompanied by the Creator, in every step, in every moment, up to infinity, unto eternity."

Anjali rejoiced in the glow of this faith.

chapter 17

Commitment

Anjali rummaged in her soul and resolved to be duty bound. Committing herself thus, she penned in her journal:

Duty-bound!
And not just the first inspirational thoughts,
But a lifelong mission persevering all battles,
A war must be conquered within,
A theme must evolve,
Delivering into an era,
Outlined by dharma,
Duties must define within,
Accountable to them alone,
I should live, Duty-bound!

Duty-bound!
In every moment, God's will be done, not mine,
Positive, happy, and with compassion abound,
Freed from fetters of the ego, his nature found,
Dismantling desire, at peace,
An inward journey begins,
As a Glass Bead Game must be played within*

* *The Glass Bead Game* is a novel by German-Swiss poet and novelist Hermann Hesse.

Duty-bound,
And ready for a journey,
The end though beautiful,
Purgatory is tough.
It must be crossed with steady steps,
Even if on cliffs, steep, severe, rocky,
But in silence and surrender,
In submission to his will, duty-bound

Duty-bound,
In quiet stillness, echoes still,
Intuitive intelligence finds its way into Tao.
All consciousness cantered into awareness,
Starts a timeless chart,
As rock-like ego melts into his grace.

Duty-bound,
Into his hands, a submission, a surrender, a joy,
Into his palms, my heart
No journey can be without him,
No happiness without,
No luxury rest its due,
In his care, freedom abounds.

Heat melts into warmth,
Scorches into sunshine
Gross into sublime,
Ambition into serenity
The sound of the flute mellows the journey,
Into a cosmic dance all elements combine,
In bonded forms, in boundless esteem, and beyond,
All duty-bound!

All horizons lose meaning,
Space and words into soft silence echo,
Time ceases to be relative.
Rhythms journey beyond creation,
The Creator rules into eternity,
Into a timeless infinity,
Beyond creation,
Yet, binding himself, remains duty-bound!

Inspirational lines in silent space echo,
"A festival of smiles, no moment my own,
Remember momentary crane, thou must fly all alone."
Celebrating life, surrendering moments,
I must fly alone,
But, duty-bound.

Forgoing all temporary delight,
Withstanding all egocentric might,
Carefully making a foundation,
That on judgment day withstands the test,
Standing undaunted in God's yard,
Speaking, and playing music like God's bard,
Duty-bound.

Duty-bound,
Invoking gods, guided at every step,
Yet, erring, again and again,
Then a stop,
Meditating, erasing flaws, fortifying strengths,
His glory plays, duty-bound!

In communion, love flows alive,
All attachments fall detached.

Compassion abounds,
Freed forgiveness resounds,
Enlivened, duty-bound!

Duty-bound,
Love in all splendour dissolves time,
Rejoining human souls, stretching into worship,
It flows mindless into all creation,
Vibrant, and duty-bound.

Duty-bound, summoning all strength, all fortitude to fight,
Duty-bound, bidding a win,
Duty-bound, looking beyond,
Duty-bound, controlling a will,
Duty-bound, conquering seven deadly sins,
Duty-bound, flowing low,
Duty-bound, not for my sake alone, but for all around.

Duty-bound,
Placing thou above self, fighting wishes and desires,
Striking proportions, duty-bound.

Duty-bound,
Accepting fate,
Welcoming every will of the Master,
Welcoming grace,
Allowing his touch, touching class,
Duty-bound!

Love like a mission, sanitised to the core,
Love replacing fear, love encores,
Love deepening with spirit, its joy revolves in truth,
Love resolves, duty-bound.

Duty-bound,
Natural truths never cease,
Even though a flower withers, its fragrance stays,
Its joy in eternity weighs,
Love like eternity cares, duty-bound.

Duty-bound,
Holding a sword, weighing against karmic weight, I strike,
And then encore, I strike, cutting the Gordian knot,
"Aum" the Gayatri recites,
In every cell, his music plays,
In every thought, his name,
He, alone,
Within, without, in you, in her, in him, duty-bound.

Duty bound now, Anjali felt love and peace softly flow through her. This love was not anxious, it was sincere and fulfilling. There was no fear of losing it. No fear of any competition.

Anjali had known suffering, and had begun to understand why she had suffered. The only refuge was the One, everything else was false. She now yearned for his grace. She faintly remembered the time when she had been close to him and wondered, "How could I have desired anything else?"

She repeatedly questioned the Creator, "Why did you not stop me? Why did you not tell me the truth? Why did you let me go?"

Her eyes welled with tears and her soul was in anguish. But she reminded herself of the resolution she had recently made, "If I am duty-bound, I have to put in efforts to resume my place. I must have faith."

Divine law did not allow her to desire the fruits of these efforts; her desire had to be relinquished to the divine will.

She closed her eyes and found herself gliding away to a celestial palace. The palace door was lit with a thousand suns and Anjali saw herself walking, then floating, and then entering this door. The other side revealed a huge hall with several little earthen lamps.

The earthen lamps greeted her, "We are souls who have returned home after a long exile. We suffered long and we learnt well. Now we are back and we must be on our guard."

Anjali thought their story was similar to hers. As if reading her thoughts, the little earthen lamps said, "Yes, our stories are indeed similar. We too once served God, and then felt that we were exemplary souls. This put pride in our hearts and we were condemned."

Anjali wondered, "Who has condemned them?" The lamps heard the question and replied, "Only one judge condemns us all."

Anjali wondered if the Creator had condemned them. The little earthen lamps flickered and spoke in a trembling voice, "No, no, please do not ever say that. The Creator never condemns anyone. To even hear this is blasphemy. You have a long way to go."

Anjali was angry with the judge. She wondered if she knew him. A little earthen lamp replied, "You must search to know who the judge is. You will find out in time."

Just then, she heard someone call out, "Anjali, Anjali!" She opened her eyes. Her mother was sitting by her side and Anjali was running a high fever. She had immersed herself in her studies and had exhausted herself with work. She had not slept for many days and her body was fatigued.

Anjali recovered soon and returned to her duties with the resolve to once again be duty-bound.

chapter 18

Interface

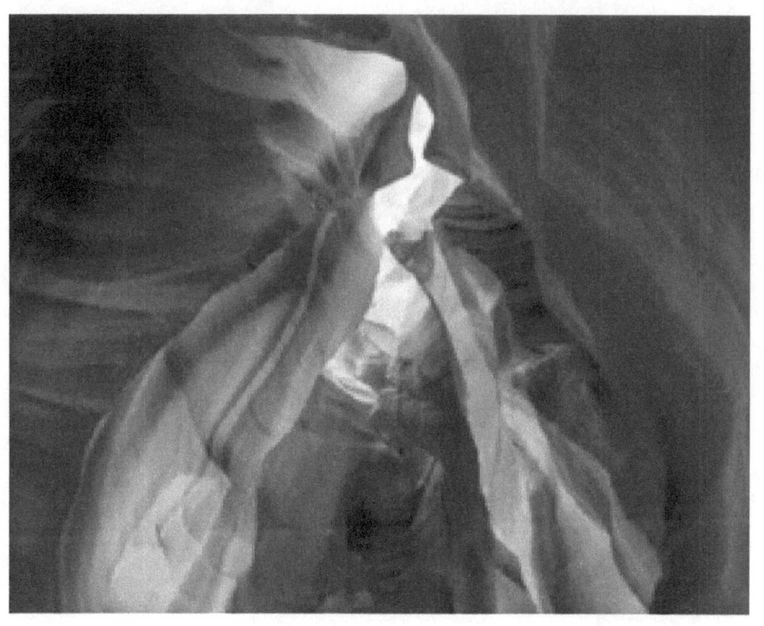

Anjali was working on the structures of power in society and the transaction costs of the politics of power. She was conducting her research on power dynamics and the changes in the rules of this game, across civilizations, through time. She studied the dynamics of power that had created and destroyed civilizations. She found that the rules of the power game became increasingly complicated and confusing as history moved on. She learnt that history not only repeats itself but also moves in a spiral, as these rules became more sophisticated and increasingly crooked.

She noted:

Yet, history also moved,
Marked by men who lived ahead of their times,
Conquering worlds, yet bloodlessly,
Made revolutions happen, yet without a sound,
Unleashed a force greater than human limits.

Liberating mankind from bondages,
Fortifying time with their images,
These men with courage and conviction ruled humankind.

Among these also lived Lilliputians,
Who measuring time with coffee spoons,
Measured steps with broken breaths.
In insignificance they lit a torch,
These proles slaved aimlessly,
Laboured unceasingly,
Delivered unconditionally,
Made history remarkably,
And yet died namelessly.
All these, as autumn after autumn, trees shed their leaves,
As poison healed patients,
And death ruled over life.

As time moved on,
Each day got shorter,
The prime of life darker,
With slanders, betrayals, life got older,
More tired, more defeated,
One, two, three… infinity,
And yet death drew nearer.

Values challenged themselves,
As in onslaught the modern ape walked,
Through a matrix of value preferences,
In a matrix of actual life processes,
Here and now.
Conflicting with traditions and institutions,
The ape losing its balance,
Churned a social unrest.

In academics, more hypocrisy was spelt than ever before,
Ideals which never would work, taught hoarse,
And once again blowing in the wind,
An unknown stirring of heart called.

Soldiers marched in blind alleys of time,
Mirroring deadpan faces,
Weighing vitality against spaces,
Time walked without a face.

Emotions walked through a Victorian age,
Completing a full circle, a bit darker, a bit more worn out,
Folds, a bit sharper,
Wrinkles, a bit more defined.
Masks, yet more perfect,
Art, more distorted,
An unknown dream haunted more compellingly.

Dreams wound their way into an era, technology ruled life,
Man enslaved himself,
Desires flowed into addiction,
Not need, but greed,
Not wisdom, but knowledge,
Not meekness, but aggression,
Not humility, but naked arrogance,
Ruled life.

Life lost its ultimate wonder,
As these knowledge slaves laboured aimlessly,
They built bridges on mirages, unceasingly,
Constructed palaces on illusions, unabatedly,
Enslaved in ambitions,
Delivered only conditionally,
Each wanting a name in history, died miserably.

Life rolled on,
So also death,
And even more so, indifference.

As love lost all meaning,
Meaning was redefined.
Power became the greatest aphrodisiac,
Love lost in the dictionary, drowned,
Religion became opium to be used only by the greedy,
Cynicism ruled life.

Even as lost lights from distant stars shone,
And saints flickered namelessly.
Autumn after autumn, trees shed their leaves,
Death alone redeemed life.
Man like a robot mimicked life,
Without a soul.

Power and the desire to control others was innate in human nature, and it was a disease.

Anjali speculated, "Power corrupts! Or is it that corruption propels its use? After all, power has only one definition—it is authority misused. But power has more than just one face: a face that lures the weak, another that confuses the mind and people into submission, yet another that exploits, and still another that wants absolute control. How many more masks men must wear to be powerful?"

She realized that, "The desire for power is so fundamental that it gives rise to politics in every institution. The more I analyse power and its structures in every institution, the more I realize that human emotions are profane."

"But then, there are structures of power in nature, too. There is a definite hierarchy of power in nature. It carries the power of God. In fact, nature is in itself power," she wrote in her notes.

Anjali researched power in nature. She discovered that, "Power in nature is natural and hence somehow godly. There is no room for profane emotions. Everything operates by instinct, by a divine program. On the other hand, the hierarchy of power in society is driven by emotions of greed and by the desire to control. Even though endowed by nature, human emotions are not natural. Neither is friendship natural, nor contempt, anger, frustration, or the game of power."

Anjali further studied why the power exercised by nature is different from the power exercised by man. She analysed the translation of organic networking into societal networking. She read volumes written on this subject and dwelt on it for a long time.

One day, as Anjali sat reading Karl Marx's *Das Kapital*, she came to understand, "Every society has a structure, as well as a super structure. Power in society is based on the generation of surplus, which is not possible without exploitation." That very moment, as though struck by inspiration, she exclaimed, "Aha!"

She joyfully penned her insight, "Human beings desire power because they subconsciously know that they are devoid of it. They are always helpless before their destinies. They seek power to feel in control of their destinies. For this, they must exploit. They must exploit people around them, they must exploit human resources around them, they must generate surplus."

"But why do human beings feel they are devoid of power and control?" she mulled. As if in a flash, she got the answer, "It is because they are not tuned to nature and they lack faith. They have desires and expectations, they are ambitious and insecure. To bridge the gap, they must seek control and power and generate surplus; therefore, they must exploit. On the other hand, power is a part of nature; in fact, nature is power. Nature is God. Nature is faith. Nature is secure. The power in nature is, therefore, not exploitative. It is innate."

Anjali discovered that corruption is an inevitable product of a power that is insecure. It raises transaction costs, and it inevitably lowers satisfaction levels. The degeneration of a civilization is measured by its response to the power structures as well as its levels of corruption.

Anjali reflected, "Humans have tremendous capacity to endure adversities but the real test of their character occurs when they are given power. Over the years, humans have degenerated into a lump of insecurity and have been ruining creation, exploiting it, endeavouring to generate surplus. Each surplus leads to higher levels of insecurities and greed."

Months rolled into years as Anjali continued her research at the academy. She collected a large amount of data that led her to significant conclusions. She came to be recognized as an eminent scholar at the academy and had many papers and reports to her credit. Her aim was to get to the root of human insecurity. What caused a lack of faith?

Another 33 years passed by at the academy.

One day, as she sat listening to music at home, with the setting sun throwing vibrant colours into the sky, she wondered, "Was this my mission? For 33 years I have not questioned myself. I have worked diligently and contributed effectively. But I have been out of touch with the Master. I have not been practicing the technique of observing my breath."

Anjali turned her attention to the setting sun. A deep sadness overcame her as she saw the colours fade out in the sky. A deep red gave way to orange, pink, streaks of purple, green and finally to a golden blue. Suddenly, it was dark and the colours were gone. The night was here to stay. Anjali contemplated, "Many, many such days have bled out ever since the earth has existed. Yet, I recollect only those days I have lived in this lifetime. I have experienced the movement of time. I feel as though creation bears a large wound, which is now penetrating my heart. This is suffering. Nature suffers every day."

In that moment, Anjali saw the whole drama of creation enact itself. She saw God suffering with his creation. She saw the birth of doubt and of a thousand other emotions, of hope and finally, the birth of faith.

All these years, Anjali had not heard the footsteps of time. But there she was, finally aware of its movement.

As Anjali looked out of the window, her eyes caught the sight of the trees that had welcomed her on the first day when she had arrived at the academy. She had thought that the trees looked like jilted lovers, standing silhouetted against the half-moon adorning the sky.

She decided, "The time has come for me to leave the academy. My mission is not research. I have to find the way to deliverance."

As she made her resolve, she continued to reflect upon it.

The meeting of earth, the fire and the waters,
For, in it I see the birth of proportions.
I see the earth gifted with discipline,
The waters with serenity,
The fires with alertness,
The breathing with awareness.
I see these elements cross their swords,
On the razor's edge, across the horizon,
I see the seer.
I am the seer.
And, the bleeding stops!

Her wound began to heal. A smile curved on Anjali's lips. She was now ready to leave the academy.

chapter 19

Mindfulness

Anjali was at the monastery with the Master seated in front of her. She revealed to him in great detail all that had happened since she had last met him, over 33 years ago.

The Master spoke thus in response:

In the secrets of silence, lies the magic of Tao,
In surrender, Zen.

Both practiced with constant vigil,
And awareness,
Through alertness,
A journey starts to the roots.

Awareness builds a crucible,
Which containing all,
Churns!

In awareness,
Reality is not concealed,
Nor misinterpreted,
Therefore, it does not exploit.

Understanding leads to depths of the horizon within!

Anjali bowed to the Master and left. She was prepared to begin her next journey, a journey within herself. The last rays of the sun were setting and though it was getting dark, Anjali rejoiced at the light she felt within.

The Master arranged for her to stay in a hut on the campus of the monastery so that she could practice. She went to the hut allotted to her and settled her belongings, while a monk brought tea and buttered bread for her dinner.

She lay awake for a long time, contemplating the Master's words. She looked back at her entire life: the pain, the revelation and her years at the academy; her mother, her father, her home and her sister, Sara, who was married and well-settled; the times spent at the *kund*. She gazed at the moon adorning the sky with all its charm and assured herself, "My ship has finally anchored safely on the shores of the monastery."

Then she sat up and, under the dim light of the hut, penned in her journal:

Anchoring my ship static and secure,
All sails are tied before my journey starts again,

Sunset floods my sight,
The colours of indigo cross the shore,
I pause, for today has seen its light.

The night has passed, and another day begun,
I tie my cargo, for another journey has begun,
Memories left behind, time races on its course,
A future of dreams again,
On a journey to another shore.

'Ere the journey ends,
Joy is on its move,
I gather shells and dews,
And guard them more precious than the muse,
'Ere they melt,
'Ere sun rays dry their course.

O! Thou precious blessings of the night
O! Thou soft petals that scatter from the skies
I dream of God and hope,
I dream of dreams,
More certain than uncertain delight,
His words on my lips,
I am once again on a tide.

Swimming with my ship,
A day, a sunset, another night,
A joy, a bridge, another light,
Time passes another tide!

Dusk, and this time the storm catches a tide,
Before it's long, a whirlpool caves my boat,
I tunnel down on purpose, on will,
This path is exciting, but with little hope.

Enticed, captured, and without rope, I descend,
And though without hope,
His palms cup my breath,
He watches from another shore.

Anjali felt the wind ruffle her hair as she began to fall asleep.

That night, she slept peacefully, as though in a divine bliss. Her heart was free from all fetters. She had let go of her past and all its furies. She had set herself free.

She dreamt about unending green meadows with wild flowers—the swaying foxgloves. The prince too appeared in her dreams, but this time she felt no pain. She dreamt she was floating over her garden, as her mother, father and sister sat near the waters of the *kund*.

She was telling them:

In years of youth, I lived with vivacity and ease,
But with so little feeling inside,
The summer and spring came back again and again,
And each time I thought this was love at last.

One day, an eagle took to wings and with spring,
It did not return,
And I knew what love was at last.

In the morning, she woke up feeling as fresh as dew. She rejoiced, "Life is indeed a celebration!" She enjoyed the freshness of the morning and spoke to the dove that ventured near the door of her hut.

A new land dreamt somewhere, is found again,
A new dream lost somewhere, is found again.
A lamp is lit unto oneself,
Secrets confirm silence,
Through fire, I pass.

Since the quest is true,
And faith confirmed,
The circle forms a full circle.

She took the dove in her palms and patted it gently. It reminded her of the dove that had once brought her the prince's message. Like a bolt of lightning, she had a flashback—the message, the prince, her maddening love for him, his departure and the hope. She remembered the words of the crystal ball reader, her past birth, the betrayal, the desperation, the hospital room and the light. She lived her whole life in that one moment.

Just then, she felt a strange kind of love for the dove but this time the love was for the bird, not the prince. The dove seemed to reciprocate her love, which made her experience a fluttering joy in her heart. This was communion. She let the bird go. As she saw it fly, she saw its feathers become golden with the rays of the sun. She watched it till it disappeared into the distant skies. She felt the pain of separation that strangely seemed to relieve her. She said to herself:

I set the bird free with no hope of its return,
With pain of its departure, I am set free.

For once, I would take life in my arms,
And dare a step I never dared before.

Walk through fire,
In excruciating pain, stand cleansed.
Through purgatory, a path leads to paradise.

During her stay at the monastery, she volunteered to serve the monks and look after the garden in front of her hut.

One day, as she sat in front of the Buddha, in the big hall of the monastery, she recalled what she had often read in the scriptures, "The mind is fragile and difficult to control.

It takes years of practice and austerity to learn to control it. Mere intellectual pursuits are not enough to control the mind. They are interesting diversions that simply entertain it. Only the breath can bring awareness, detachment and non-possession. One should observe the breath with alertness and equanimity, with the knowledge deeply seeded that everything is temporary."

She bowed before the Buddha and was reminded of what the Master had once said about Buddha's instructions to his monks, "The greatest homage to me is to practice the path; the foundation is correct conduct. The path cannot be practiced without this foundation."

Walking through the corridors of the monastery, she deliberated, "The world is full of diversions and the emotions are heedless. I know it will require immense effort and constant practice before I can even attempt to tame my mind. However, I am determined, and I pray that this shall continue. Nothing can happen without God's grace."

The Master saw her pass and heralded her into his room. He asked her, "What do you seek here?" Anjali replied, "I wish to sink into nothingness. I wish to become love, the love that does not discriminate. I seek to look within myself and master my own self."

The Master smiled, "The world is a huge laboratory into which human beings are born to experiment and discover. To gain what you seek, you need to lose a lot more—your doubts, fears, insecurities and anxieties. When you are empty, faith will fill itself in you. Surrender to faith; however, surrender shall happen when you accept everyone and everything as they are."

"You are the ocean. If it rains, it makes no difference to the ocean. If it does not rain, it also makes no difference to the ocean. The ocean accepts everything and is unaffected.

It embraces all the rivers. In it, the good and the bad both find solace. This is the crux of acceptance. Acceptance comes out of surrender. Surrender to God's will. It comes with the knowledge that each moment is perfect. Whatever happens in this moment is perfect and anything else will be otherwise. Most of all, acceptance comes through an objective awareness."

He further explained, "Awareness is non-interpretative and amoralistic. Awareness gives one the advantage that a *drishta* (witness) has. The experience is like that of a lotus. The petal remains untouched by the water and everything surrounding it. This awareness has to be continuous. If the awareness is lost even for a moment, involvement creeps in and with it, the weakness of the heart. The vigil has to be constant. It cannot be let down even for a moment, even for a fraction of a second. It requires continuous practice and effort. As the awareness builds up, new horizons unfold. It leads to a centre, which has not been discovered."

The Master elaborated:

Exploring into a valley,
One needn't always look for flowers,
Entering a jungle,
One needn't always look for beasts,
Eroding mountains,
One needn't always find caves.

"You must not expect the expected. You must not try to look for things because of the preconceived training of the intellect. When you do that, you often miss out on the essential. The essential remains invisible because the mind is not trained to see it. Often, the beauties of life are lost. Often, the essence of living is missed," he concluded.

Day after day, Anjali practiced meditation. Day after day, the Master shared with her invaluable wisdom.

"To accept," he once explained, "one has to de-condition oneself and return to the original condition of a child who plays in the mud. The child does not discriminate between the clean and the unclean, the good and the bad. The child's mind is pure and innocent, untouched by conditions."

The Master taught Anjali how to communicate with her subconscious, how to talk to the plants and how to reach the superconscious mind. On one occasion, he told her, "Every person has a child within them. This child is pure, innocent, divine. Therefore, this child can access the superconscious mind and through it, the ultimate consciousness. In the solitude of the space within, any person can communicate with this innate intuitive self and ask for answers. It can unravel the mysteries of nature." However, he warned Anjali, "This science should be used discretely and only for the good of others. There are principles to be observed. Any wrong use could cause a spiritual downfall!"

Anjali often practiced concentrating on her breath while walking. During one such walk, she came across a huge well, which the monks often talked about. Stories abounded about the discovery of this well. Some said that for many years the monastery had faced a water crisis and nobody could find an answer to it. Since the monastery was at a height, nobody knew of any spot where water could be struck. Then, the spot appeared in the Master's dream and a huge unending source of water was found there. Others said that the Master had seen the water with his mind's eye. Some mentioned that at the time of a merciless drought in the area, the Master had prayed unceasingly for 40 days. The god of rain had descended from the heavens and given the Master a pitcher full of water. The Master had placed the pitcher on the ground and immediately the ground sucked in the pitcher. The Master had that spot dug up and water was discovered there. The god of rain had told the Master that the water in the pitcher would never dry up. Indeed, ever since the supply of water had nourished the needs of all the villages around the monastery for years and years.

That evening, Anjali asked the Master to tell her about the well. The Master revealed, "I had discovered the well by invoking the answer from the child within me. The child within revealed exactly where the water could be found as well as its exact depth. My innate intuitive self guided me through this search. Thus, the well manifested."

The Master informed her, "To reach the truth, every element on the way has to be perfect. The communication should be perfect, the intentions should be selfless, the inner child should be healed so that the innate intuitive self can manifest itself. The pendulum has to be perfectly balanced."

In the days that followed, Anjali realized that the working of nature is perfect and perfection balances itself delicately. Sensitivity and stability are precariously proportioned. Nature is in a state of perfect mindfulness. It is constantly alert and vigilant. Nature evolves in this mindfulness. It plays in this mindfulness and procreates in this mindfulness. That is why everything in nature is in perfect harmony. That is why nature is in a constant celebration. And that is why everything operates in nature effortlessly."

The Master's presence and the monastery's environment were steadily showing her a new dimension of existence, which was mindful, vigilant and enlightened. She felt the power of this existence and the tremendous freedom it gave her.

Awestruck, she wrote in her journal:

On stairways winding into blind alleys of heart,
In mists of memory lanes,
In wilderness of echoes growing fainter, inching into time,
Space melts into music,
And how the soul reaches out!

In this orchestra I feel,
Friends, faces, lost hopes no longer disturb,
A continuum stretches into a subconscious,
The Supreme Being distils peace.

One evening, Anjali expressed her gratitude to the Master for all his guidance. His reply came in the form of a warning, "You are making a mistake. You attach much importance to words. Words do not mean anything. They create an illusion. You again fetter your soul. It is a paradox. You must be a light unto yourself. Even a small lamp is more worthy than the moon that shines only by the light of the sun. The lamp is a light unto itself."

The Master gently rebuked her, "You transferred your emotional dependence on your mother, on the prince, and now you are transferring it onto me."

He warned her:

Watch!
Again fetters begin to play a lure,
Freedom takes to flight,
Infatuation pursues like never before.
An unfettered soul is chained!

Anjali realized the wisdom in these words. She was grateful to the Master for not wanting her to depend on him, and for manoeuvring her onto the path of the light, which would set her free.

Anjali said:

Comparing thus with thee,
Helpless, and without control,
In search, and without meaning,
Deafened, blinded, killed,
Alas, truth comes to rescue.

The path is now known.
In mindful surrender,
Like a lamp unto oneself,
Enlightenment lights the way.

Sculpturing poetry on a stone,
The soul surrenders,
Liberated by the Master's love.

Anjali sat in front of the Master for a long time, watching her breath and absorbing the benefits of his presence. The layers of karma that shrouded her existence were peeling away one by one. As each layer fell away, she got closer to being liberated from her mortal destiny. She felt increasingly close to God and yearned for him, more than she had ever before.

chapter 20

Paradox

In realization,
I witness an event,
No longer fragile,
This play of ego.

I witness it again and again,
Changeless, robust, resistant,
It rises again and again,
I witness it once again,
The ego, feeling my eye,
Attempts to shy,
I witness it again.

No noise is heard,
No sight is lost,
Is the ego dead?
Or feigning death, would it rise once again?

Anjali experienced this strange play of her ego. She watched her breath and her thoughts, and each time she observed them, she felt *its* presence. She had read in one of the scriptures, "Subtler than the mind is the intellect; subtler than the intellect, the ego."

She once observed during her meditation, "The 'I' temporarily retreats to the background and then reemerges stronger. It has always been *my* breath, *my* thoughts and *my* concentration."

Anjali continued her practice, day after day, with the same effort. Month after month, year after year… even a lifetime was not enough to master the practice. Seven years passed by at the monastery.

The routines of the monastery and her continuous practice kept her busy. She conversed with the monks whenever they found time, and the Master shared his knowledge with her. Anjali was slowly learning to observe her breath mindfully, dispassionately and with alertness. Her practice was becoming more stable. Her old passions were giving way to the objectivity that awareness brings. Anjali observed that she was becoming more compassionate. She could empathize with the pain and suffering of people around her. She could understand the suffering of every living creature. "Is this suffering a projection of my mind?" she wondered.

One thing was certain, she no longer thought only about herself—neither about her needs nor her suffering. She could find herself in the hopes, dreams and wishes of all.

Once, she asked the Master, "How is it that, at one time, I had been consoled by the suffering of people who suffered more than I did?"

The Master replied, "Because you were insecure, and you did not have enough faith in yourself."

Anjali wondered, "Was I being selfish when I did not want others to get what I had been deprived of?"

The Master explained, "That is human nature. It is foolish. Humans are deluded when they consider themselves separate from others. They are unaware that they are part of the same rhythm; that they are interdependent. In fact, all their hopes, dreams and desires are interdependent, and so are their happiness and sorrow. The sorrows of others only add to the total unhappiness of humankind. Humans, by making others unhappy, add to their own unhappiness. Humans build false boundaries and suffer immensely."

Anjali reflected, "What you say is true. We are so alienated from this universal rhythm that we feel secure when others are insecure and unhappy. We compare ourselves with others, and we are happy if others are less happy. We compare our looks, our possessions, our achievements, our knowledge, our vigour, our associations, our status in society, our way of thinking, our worldviews, we even compare our faiths. We live a relative existence. However, we certainly do not rejoice when others are better off than we are, or even if we perceive them to be better off than we are."

The Master explained, "Nothing can be more disastrous than comparison. Comparison is of no consequence since every creation is unique—that is the beauty of creation. Even identical twins, with the same genetic code, are unique in themselves. They have their separate missions, separate destinies. God is original. He never repeats himself. The law of karma operates in everyone's life, and it decides and determines everything that is to come."

The Master added, "It is foolish to compare because everyone's destiny is predetermined. Intense effort alone can change your destiny. Just as you can change the future, you can change your past, but for that you must suffer. You must live through suffering, know suffering, and then enjoy suffering. You must suffer to the fullest. Any dilution will only add to the burden of your karmas."

"Suffering is a great opportunity to change your past. You must therefore learn to celebrate suffering," the Master explained.

"Every action adds to the burden of your karmas. Even comparing yourself with others adds to this karma. It is not a positive act. Help others achieve their goals and your goals will be reached automatically." After a brief pause, he asked Anjali, "But do you know what the catch in this is?"

Anjali tried to guess, "The catch is that you may lose the ambition to have a goal."

The Master smiled, "No, the catch is that if you help others achieve their goals in the hope that nature will help you achieve your own goals, you will fail. You have to perform every action with unconditional commitment and absolute selflessness."

The Master continued, "The intention should be pure. Nature watches every intent. Only when actions are done without motive or consideration for results can they produce the right effect. Then alone they attract divine grace."

Anjali thought, "That is difficult indeed."

"Nature is subtle," the Master explained, "and it operates on subtleties. It considers your intentions more than your actions. Any action tainted with a hidden motive is suspect. Nature sees it as an act to deceive. Nature does not like deception."

Anjali enquired, "Do you suggest that inaction is better than action done with a motive?"

The Master clarified, "Even inaction is an action since a person acted by not acting when he could have acted. Action is necessary; more so if the action is in pursuit of your assigned duties. Not acting in pursuit of your assigned duties adds to the burden of your karmas. In fact, inaction is worse than action done with a motive because inaction is dishonest both in form and spirit."

The Master asked Anjali, "Do you know why you suffered for so long?"

She thoughtfully replied, "Yes, I suffered because of my desire and longing. I suffered because I wanted to possess the object of my desire."

The Master questioned her again, "Do you know what this desire to possess means?"

Anjali was silent. Without waiting for an answer he continued, "It only means that you want to control something or someone. You want to lay claim on another person's life and control it. You suffered because you thought that you could control, first your destiny and then the prince. Nature controls, you do not control. You control only your suffering and you squandered your sufferings in vain poetry. Life is not a gift. It is a loan to you, which you must pay back in full measure. Measure for measure, without waste; dust to dust, gold to gold."

Anjali asked, "Does a mother have no claim over the child she begets? Does a lover have no claim over his beloved? Does a devotee have no claim over his God? Does a disciple have no claim over his guru?"

The Master smiled, "The social relationships only disguise associations of previous births. Some of these associations may even surprise you. Do you know a father and a son could have been enemies in their previous birth? And in the present, they distress each other endlessly. Their love may be full of anxiety and revenge, their actions could be causing endless pain to each other. The father loves his son because he thinks he gave him birth. He thinks that he created him in some way, that he is his blood. Nothing can be further from the truth. God alone creates."

The Master continued, "Even a mother's love for her son is selfish. Her son is her extended ego. Every person is born to outlive his destiny. But the father, thinking himself the cause, feels responsible and invests all his resources in his son. This only adds to his attachment and arrogance. He then wants to control his son's destiny. His son in turn feels it his right to have everything he asks for. The son invests little in the relationship, and feels less committed to the relationship. One day he leaves. This causes the father much pain and suffering, and the revenge is complete. The debts of a previous birth are recovered."

"The beauty is that nature disguises hostility with love. No one realizes that it is revenge, with much pain and suffering."

Anjali asked, "Are all close relationships born similarly, or could they have different roots?"

The Master replied, "Yes, there are some positive relationships also, but such relationships are few. They are born out of pure love in the past. Such relationships do not cause concern or anxiety, and are not possessive. They flow with nature. These relationships are crafted with deep insight. Such relationships help either of the persons in every way. They enrich one emotionally, intellectually and, most importantly, spiritually. Such relationships never cease, even if one of the persons dies."

As the conversation progressed, a monk ran up and spoke nervously to the Master. The Master got up immediately, went to his cottage, closed the door and returned after a few minutes. He was ready to leave for a trip. He asked Anjali to pack some clothes and accompany him, and they set off, along with the two monks who were waiting at the monastery gates.

It was a long journey through the illusion of shifting landscapes. This was the first time she had exited the gates of the monastery since she entered it seven years ago. The outside world seemed so different from what she had left behind before joining the monastery.

As she was enjoying the views outside, Anjali glanced at the Master. He seemed to have gone deep within himself, into the sanctum sanctorum of his heart. He was immersed in his prayers. She wondered, "Why is a part of me so relieved to be on this journey with the Master?"

chapter 21

Death

As the bus came to a halt, Anjali opened her eyes. They had arrived at a small town. She followed the Master through narrow lanes lined with houses till they reached a poor man's cottage. It was made of mud and had a wooden door. The Master knocked on the door and without waiting for anyone to answer, he walked in. He signalled Anjali and the two monks to wait in the veranda while he entered the room. The veranda had wooden windows and four chairs, two with broken arms. The Master's photograph adorned one of the walls with a small earthen lamp lit beneath it. This added grace and beauty to the little veranda.

A slender teenage girl came out from the inner room of the cottage and told Anjali to accompany her into the room. Inside, she saw a critically ill man lying on a bed. Anjali wondered who this man was, considering that the Master was in such a hurry to see him. The Master was seated next to the man. He was immersed in his prayers. On the other side were the man's wife and a young boy who did not seem older than 12.

Anjali looked around the room and her eyes fell on a photograph hanging on the wall. It was a photograph of the prince. She then looked at the dying old man on the bed. His features resembled those of the prince. She wondered, "This man seems to be related to the prince. Could this be his father or maybe his older brother? Where is the prince?"

The Master knew what Anjali was thinking. He looked at her, nodded and let out a chuckle. Anjali was more confused. "The old man is dying and the Master is chuckling!" she thought. Anjali had never seen the Master like this; he always wore a serious expression. And since they had left the monastery, his seriousness had acquired a sombre expression.

Anjali kept glancing at the Master. He looked her straight in the eye and, in a flash, Anjali figured it out. "The dying man is the prince!" Pain pierced her heart as she realized this.

She looked back at the dying man and wondered, "What has become of him, and how?" She had first seen the prince in all his grandeur in the glass mountain. She had dreamt of him many times and had always seen him surrounded by luxuries. She had seen him walk on the richest carpets and ride the best of horses. "What happened to all of that? Here lies the prince in abject poverty. He looks more like a shadow of the prince I have known. Forty years have passed since I saw him last. His face lacks the charm and grace that always adorned him. However, I do see repentance written large upon it," she thought.

Anjali knew that the prince was reaching the end of the number of breaths in his account, and was waiting for the Master to arrive so that he could breathe his last.

His wife was inconsolable and Anjali went to her to comfort her. The woman neither welcomed Anjali's gesture nor rejected it. She was oblivious to all that was happening around her as she stood there with her two grandchildren, watching her husband dying.

Anjali broke into tears. The old man opened his eyes and, as he saw the Master, he tried to get up but he was too weak to do so. The Master told him to keep resting. The man wished to speak to the Master privately. The Master gestured all to leave the room. The two men spent four hours together while Anjali waited outside, impatiently.

Anjali wondered if the Master would heal the old man. She looked at the young children and the man's wife and felt deep sympathy for them. She had already lived through all the emotions of pain, yet she felt hurt waiting there with the prince's wife. However, this pain seemed to be liberating. Anjali felt lighter somehow. She wondered, "Are there any more emotions I need to live out in my association with this man? He is no longer the prince I had pined for. I had all along deluded myself. I had bound myself to vain desires and a longing that has no reality."

Everything was now clear to her. "The prince was never mine; there probably had never been a prince to begin with." Having suffered an excruciating pain, Anjali had outlived it. The only emotion she felt now was compassion. She sincerely hoped and prayed for the family.

Anjali was lost in her thoughts when she heard the Master giggling inside the room.

She pondered, "How do people continue to suffer despite the powers nature has gifted them? Maybe a person has to outlive his destiny before he can realize he has the power to change it. This realization alone is not enough. The real effort is discipline, which makes this effort possible—the *iron will* to observe it."

"The secret is to outlive all desires. The secret is to know that the pleasant and the unpleasant, the good and the bad, the loved and the hated, the pleasurable and the painful are all the same. All is temporary and hence without substance," she speculated.

"Living life is like walking on a razor's edge. The razor is always ready to strike, always ready to make us bleed, always ready to test, always ready to reverse the journey, and it is the only way to cut the karmas."

The Master then called Anjali inside. She went in and saw the prince had only a few breaths remaining. He looked at her as though seeking forgiveness. The Master asked Anjali to sit and observe her breath. He then called the man's family inside. As Anjali sat and observed her breath, she saw herself on the sands of the Sahara. Her mind narrated:

Dust hitting your face,
Endless space of emptiness,
Yet beautiful.

Rich in solitude,
Conquering souls that search,
These sands of Sahara,
Savouring eternity.

Blood drying with heat,
Molten lava flowing from hearts,
You see the Master on the sands of Sahara.

chapter 22

Dissolution

Anjali woke up in her home. "How is this possible?" she wondered. She saw Sara sitting by her side, a serious look on her face. Her mother was seated on the other side, looking as though she had had far too many sleepless nights. Anjali speculated, "Have I been unconscious for many hours or many days? Did they think I was dead?"

She recalled, "I had seen the man, who I thought was my prince, die. I remember the sands of the Sahara. I also remember the Master standing next to me. I remember the doctor. I remember that I remembered no more."

She looked at Sara and her mother again. A calming breeze caressed her face, lulling her back to sleep.

Anjali was moving through the cosmos full of stars and galaxies, across the entire breadth of the universe. She moved on, into an endless eternity. It was neither dark nor light. Time stood still and then, as if in a second, billions of years rolled in.

She saw herself in a room with little earthen lamps. The lamps were talking to each other and she heard them mention her name many times. Then there were whispers as someone hushed them.

Anjali saw each lamp moving in its own trajectory, charting its own destiny; and yet, they were all mystically and eternally connected. Anjali moved via innumerable beings. She observed:

Millions in a rush,
Thousands aspiring,
Only a very few truly moving.

Moving and longing,
Longing for something,
Maybe for the One.

Each soul on its journey,
Thousands resisting,
Many questioning,
Still more challenging it.

Each living its own destiny,
Some outliving it,
Yet none changing it.

In tune, or out of it,
They all lived it.

They cross many-a-mire,
Yet a mire remains within.
Traversing ten thousand lives,
Outliving a thousand heartbreaks,
They journey through.

Was Anjali going on her last journey? A journey into herself? As she wondered, her journey reversed. She entered back into the universe.

The vain moon was complaining, "My attachment to the sun has ruined my beauty. Look at the blemish on my beautiful face. It is all the sun's doing."

The sun was carping too, "It was you who first betrayed my trust. I loved you and you walked away with the earth. My heart has been aflame ever since."

The moon confessed, "I shall shine because of the love I carry for you in my heart."

The sun replied, "No, you shine because of my light, the light from my heart which is ablaze. I am slowly wearing out in this fire."

The moon retorted, "Even if you wear out this way, you will be remembered forever. After all, all life exists because of this fire in your heart."

The little earthen lamps explained to Anjali, "There is frequent bickering among the sun, moon and earth; also among all the stars, planets and their moons. They question each other's relative imperfections, even though each one is, in fact innately perfect. All this happens only because of ignorance."

The earthen lamps continued, "Everything is interdependent, everything exists because of each other and for each other. Everything has a purpose. Even the blemish on the moon has a purpose and certainly; the fire in the sun has a purpose. Nothing exists separately, nothing exists in itself. A master string of life permeates all existence. All communications are, therefore, powerful and subtle. The subconscious of all elements, of all beings and also of all things forms a giant ocean in which the gods bathe. From this ocean of subconscious emerges all creation. One has to be alert to the thoughts. The trick is to hear them enter and watch them so that one is not carried away by them."

The wise earthen pots reiterated, "One has to be alert all the time. Alert to the thoughts, the breath, existence itself, life, death and above all, alert to the grace that so continuously flows." The flames in the earthen pots continued, "You must watch your breath. This helps improve your concentration. Never let your vigil drop. That is the secret. But beware of the invisible judge."

Anjali listened attentively. She knew she had to be alert, and alert all the time, but she wondered, "How? And who is this judge?"

The earthen lamps read her thoughts and instructed her: "Go watch your breath; if you do it well, you will know who the judge is."

Anjali had been watching her breath all these years but she had not discovered this judge. Anjali enquired again. The earthen lamps replied, "Guard against yourself." Anjali failed to understand what they meant. She requested them to explain but they simply swayed.

She then questioned the winds that fanned the flames in the little earthen pots.

The winds answered, "The winds shall obey his will. We obey his will. We obey *only* his will."

Anjali was determined to know the answer. She questioned the earth, the sun, the ether, the air, the water and the fire.

She suddenly saw the faces she had seen in the asylum. She heard them crying out, "Do not disturb us. We carry a great responsibility. Do not disturb us."

Then she heard them cry in greater pain, "We are condemned."

She asked again, "Who has condemned you?"

They replied, "A judgment is passed. We are condemned."

She enquired again, "Who is this judge?"

The faces disappeared. The winds roared. She felt her breath becoming fainter and fainter. She saw a long forgotten drama once again. She saw the dew drops robed in sunshine meet at his feet.

Fragile though the act would seem,
It was significant,
An angel was born.

I see the entire stage clearly now,
In the stillness of a moment,
Planets switch their roles.
A lull before a storm,
A lull after one,
The sweet angel graces,
In submission, drops its wings.

Flight, a symbol of the ego,
Was dropped down at his feet,
Fragile, once again, that act though seemed,
It was significant.

An angel is reborn
Remembering the One,
The only One,
Connecting within.

Anjali heard a thumping sound. The whole place was transformed into a majestic court. The judge entered. Anjali waited to see the face. At last, she would know who the judge is. The judge turned towards the court and Anjali stood in the trial box. But the judge was veiled. Anjali said to herself, "Alas, the judge hides his face. And I know why."

She waited for the judge to question her. The judge paused, the veil fluttered in the wind. Anjali tried to guess. The judge looked familiar, very familiar. And lo and behold, in another moment, Anjali found herself seated as the judge. From trial box to the judge's pedestal, and from the judge's pedestal to the trial box and back, and back and forth, Anjali saw herself at both the places. Anjali the accused looked at Anjali the judge, even as Anjali the judge looked to pass judgment on Anjali the accused. Each stared at the other, face to face. The stare seemed endless and daunting.

Once again, Anjali witnessed the game of the mirrors.

Between mirrors,
The possessor became the possessed,
Seen, the object.

Between mirrors,
The creator became the created,
Created, its creator.

The witness stands unmoved,
Knowing the unreality of all.

All emotions died. All judgments perished. Anjali discovered that nothing had been, nothing was. It was unreal all along. There was no right, no wrong. No good, no evil, no silence, no noise, no colours, neither darkness nor light. Nothing ever has been. No universe, no space, no time, no misleading black holes. Nothing ever was, nothing ever could be. It was the 'I' that created this illusion. It was the 'I' that judges, the 'I' that condemns, and the 'I' that causes all suffering. 'I' was the enemy, the very 'I' that was within; constantly within, even as it was constantly fed, nurtured and spoiled.

The bards played the sweetest melody; the drama of her life on earth was replayed for her to see.

In a moment she saw herself and heard herself whisper:

Revelling in human love,
I find myself struggling in the human womb,
Thro' human love,
This sweet angel prays.

I think this is the path,
Thro' his heart,
Thro' his eyes,
To know his love,
To see his first ray of sunshine,
Thro' him, to be born in his eyes.

Alas, human love is frail,
In frailty, it betrays,
A tear in my eyes,
I surrender all hope.

Sorrow pins my soul,
Forgiveness has no part.
Fires dance on water,
Yet they do not burn.

Love hurts,
And hurt burns.

Pained, I watch, in pain,
As I witness the play of the ego.

In ego, I struggle,
Smothered, in chains,
I fight this time for survival.

The chains clasp around me with a tighter grip,
Tighter and tighter, yet tighter,
I choke, I struggle, yet more,
Am I dead?

Assuming death, I surrender.
The game is lost,
Or so I think.
The ego surrenders to a pattern.

I pause,
I wonder,
I rewind the game,
Playing it forward and backward,
I hear the music,
I hear the song,
I see the planets.

I witness an event,
No longer fragile,
This play of ego,
I witness it again and again,
Reminding me of "Raktabīja"

Ego touching the earth, feeling the mud,
Springs again, strengthened.

I waive it off!
Like a dragon, it waves its head,
Regaining confidence.

Surfacing again, yet again,
And alive, connected to life,
I kill it again and again, and once again.
The ego feeling my eyes,
Attempts to shy.

Yet staring me in the face,
The ego returns my gaze.

Its teeth are bared into sharpened corners,
Like a blade, it springs its head to attack!

This time I do not judge,
Nor waive it off,
Nor invite it.

Ignored,
Paralysed,
The invisible judge loses teeth.
It cannot condemn!

A mirror breaks,
The winds smoothen into zephyrs,
The fires arrange into evening stars.
Stormy oceans lull the ships,
The shore is nigh.

No noise is heard,
No sight lost,
As an ego fades.

This time,
No angel is born.
Yet, far away in a void,
Music is heard.

Anjali floated into the great void. The winds bellowed vigorously. The lights played around the cosmic prism. All the angels bowed, even as the angel of death stood without a role.

Between mirrors,
The created became the Creator,
The Creator and its creation.

Love endears like a lightning collapsing all dimensions into the One!

About the Author

Kavita Gupta is a top bureaucrat from the Indian Administrative Service (1985 Batch, Maharashtra Cadre) and has a long and variegated experience in administration. She has made outstanding and innovative contributions in her multifarious assignments.

She has navigated her spiritual journey through streams of all major religious thoughts. She has studied under the guidance of many masters during the process. Constantly in search of the truth, she has learnt and practiced various spiritual techniques.

She has, all along, pursued and excelled in academics. She has a PhD. in International Economics from Prescott University, London, and four master's degree: Masters in Physics with credits in Engineering from Indian Institute of Technology, Delhi; M.Tech in Behavioural and Social Sciences, again from IIT Delhi; Masters in International Law and International Economics from the World Trade Institute, Berne, Switzerland (awarded summa cum laude). She studied at the Harvard Kennedy School, USA, and was awarded a certificate in "Infrastructure in a Market Economy, Public-Private Partnerships in a Changing World." She has also successfully completed a certificate program in "Negotiations for Public Leaders" at the University of California, Berkeley, USA, and a certificate course on "Women Mean Business" from Durham University Business School, UK. She is a certified yoga instructor from Aatmabodh Academy of Yoga, Mumbai, in association with Ayush Medical Association, India, and affiliated with World Academy of Traditional Science, Rishikesh, Uttarakhand. Importantly, she is also a preceptor in "The Heartfulness Way" of meditation and is trained to practice past life regression therapy, inner child therapy, family constellation therapy, mastering breathwork, traversing the frequencies and creating a psychic shield. Further, she is also a tarot card reader.